A TRAILS

COUNTY PARKS
OF MINNESOTA

300 Parks You Can Visit
Featuring 25 Favorites

TIMOTHY J. ENGRAV

TRAILS BOOKS
Black Earth, Wisconsin

Library of Congress Control Number: 2005927137
ISBN: 1-931599-60-2

Editor: Mark Knickelbine
Photos: Timothy J. Engrav
Designer: Kathie Campbell
Cover Photo: Michael Shedlock
Maps: Magellan Mapping Company

Printed in the United States of America by Versa Press, Inc.
10 09 08 07 06 05   6 5 4 3 2 1

TRAILS BOOKS, a division of Trails Media Group, Inc.
P.O. Box 317 • Black Earth, WI 53515
(800) 236-8088 • e-mail: books@wistrails.com
www.trailsbooks.com

To my wife, Kristen, and our children, Abbigail and Alexander; thank you for your love, support, and patience.

Minnesota Counties

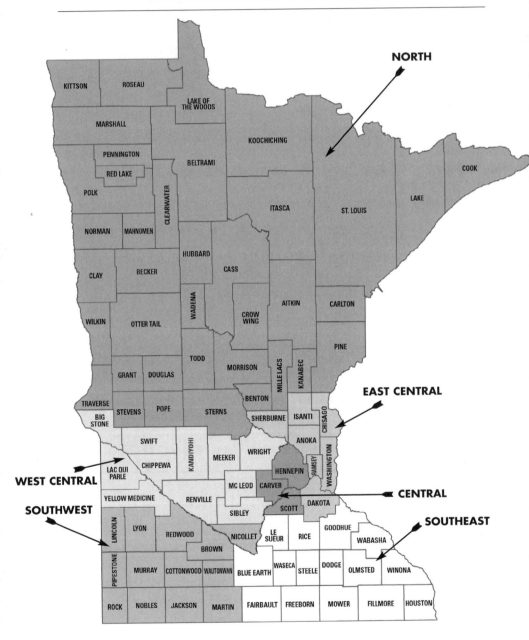

Contents

25 Favorite County Parks   1

Some Favorite Parks for Special Uses   31

Guide to County Parks   41

NORTH REGION

WEST-CENTRAL REGION

Introduction

My interest and devotion to county parks in Minnesota stems from the years I worked as the Park and Recreation Director for Itasca County. This experience gave me first hand knowledge of the state's county parks and the treasures and value that they hold. I was also able to rely on my professional knowledge of park management and maintenance in order to provide accurate, quality descriptions of these parks.

The variety of Minnesota's natural beauty is a wondrous thing, and much of it can be observed within its 310 county parks. This notion was continually reinforced as I crisscrossed the state, visiting almost every county and observing hundreds of parks. I enjoyed watching the change in topography and landscapes from north to south and east to west. When my family could come along, we made it an adventure; when I went solo I covered as many miles as I could. What I saw only reaffirmed my sense of pride in Minnesota and its residents. I was and still am thrilled to have had the opportunity to write this book and contribute something that I hope is useful for enjoying county parks in the great state of Minnesota.

The experience has also shown me the importance and significance of local efforts to preserve and protect parks. So many of these special areas would not have been designated had it not been for the efforts of local citizens and elected officials who recognized the need to protect these places and provide locations for outdoor enjoyment. I commend and thank all of those dedicated individuals and encourage others to get involved. Open space, parks, and recreation serve to strengthen the soul and refresh the spirit.

During my seven years of working in outdoor recreation and park management in Minnesota, I have visited hundreds of county parks, experiencing them in all types of weather and keeping notes on what they have to offer. From these travels I do have some favorites, and so I have put together a list of them and why I think that they are special in the section "Twenty-Five Favorite Parks." In addition, many people are always on the lookout for destinations for specific recreation opportunities like camping, winter recreation, historical sites, and the like. In "Some Favorite Parks for Special Uses," I have listed what I consider to be the best local parks in the state for these activities and others. These sections offer additional insight into the beauty, charm, and variety of Minnesota's county parks.

I hope that readers will find this book useful and practical. While most of the guidebook should be self-explanatory, the reader may benefit from some explanation of a few of the book's key elements.

ACCESSIBILITY

Handicap-accessible facilities are very important, because they allow people of all abilities to enjoy the benefits of our parks. Today, when recreation facilities are designed and built, they must meet the accessibility standards of the Americans with Disabilities Act of 1990 and subsequent amendments. Many of the existing county park facilities were built before 1990, and while several facilities have been built since 1990, over time the regulations have been adapted and changed. What this means is that when you visit Minnesota's county parks, you will experience different types of accessibility, mainly based on when a park facility was built. If a facility was designated as handicap-accessible, I note it as handicap-accessible in the book's description of the facility. While I have tried my best to provide accessibility information, if you have concerns or questions about the handicap-accessibility at a specific park, I encourage you to contact the responsible department for more detailed information.

SEASONS

As I visited parks, I gathered information about when parks and campgrounds are open to visitors. Some parks have very specific dates of operation, others are open year-round, and others are generally open and closed based on the weather. During the winter, parks with flexible dates may be closed by gates or become inaccessible because of a lack of snowplowing. Many counties will base the opening and closing of these parks on the first snowfall of winter and the final melt of spring. When the exact dates of opening and closing vary, I have listed the seasons as May through September or April through October. Some parks also provide lake access during the summer and winter seasons. Again, if you are planning a trip in the early spring or late fall and need specific information, call the county listed (the book provides contact information for each location).

DEFINITIONS

Most of the county-owned parks in Minnesota are designated as parks or county parks. However, in the Twin Cities area, the Metropolitan Regional Park

System, which includes six counties and the Three Rivers Park District, uses two additional park titles and definitions. In addition, several nonmetro counties are also beginning to use these park titles.

Park or County Park: Designated areas of various sizes operated by a county government that offer a variety of recreation opportunities.

Regional Park: Designated areas of 100 to 500 acres operated by a county government that offer a wide range of outdoor recreation opportunities.

Park Reserve: Designated areas of 1,000 or more acres operated by a county government that offer a wide range of outdoor recreation opportunities. At least 80 percent of a park reserve must remain undeveloped in order to protect and preserve representative landscapes.

DIRECTIONS

I have tried my best to provide detailed directions to all of the parks. However, I recommend keeping a good map or atlas available, such as the *Minnesota Atlas and Gazetteer* published by DeLorme.

Finally, I have made every effort to ensure the accuracy of information provided in this guidebook; but if you notice errors or omissions, please write to me: Timothy Engrav, c/o Minnesota County Parks, Trails Media Group, Inc., PO Box 317, Black Earth, WI 53515.

I would like to express my thanks to Trails Books for the opportunity to share my enthusiasm for Minnesota's glorious local parks. And I extend sincere thanks to all of the state's county park departments for their valuable help during this project. Best wishes to you on your county park adventure!

Minnesota Counties

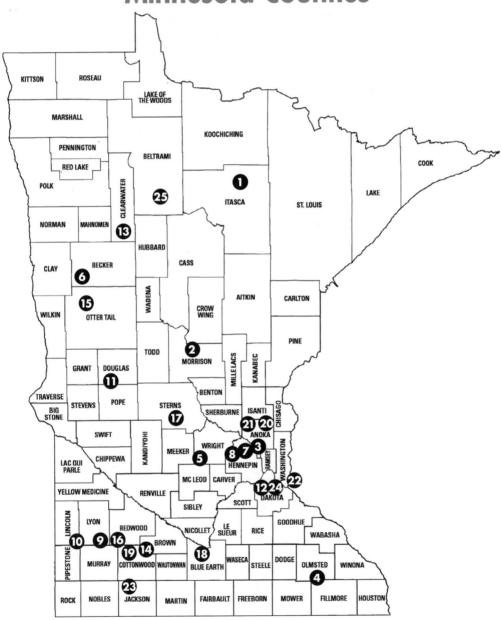

25
FAVORITE COUNTY
PARKS

More information on each of these parks is available in the "Guide to County Parks" section.

1. Bass Lake County Park

Itasca County
(218) 327-2855
www.co.itasca.mn.us

Hidden in the northeast corner of Itasca County, Bass Lake County Park offers an enchanting experience for camping, picnicking, fishing, and hiking in a wilderness-like setting. The landscape includes over 700 acres of pine, balsam, and aspen forest; several wetlands; and four main lakes. The very remote atmosphere, more than 40 miles from the closest large city, Grand Rapids, is definitely part of the charm of this park.

All of the developed facilities are located on Bass Lake, including a primitive-style campground that can accommodate RVs and tents, a small beach, an open picnic area, a small-boat ramp, and a short hiking trail. Bass Lake and three other lakes provide pan fish and the elusive bass, with fishing opportunities from the shore or small boats. Swimming and relaxation are also popular lakeside pastimes. The campground's most attractive feature is that there is not a bad campsite in the place. In fact, every campsite is located on the lakeshore.

During my first visit, the beautiful forest and lake setting reminded me of the Boundary Waters Canoe Area Wilderness so much so that, if not for the motor vehicles and boats, I would have completely forgotten where I was. Subsequent visits to the park have included several opportunities for quiet and solitude. There is something special about the majestic red and white pines that flank the shoreline of the park's namesake lake. Here's hoping that the rustic charm of the campground will remain long into the future.

Directions: *From Grand Rapids, take Highway 169 north to Nashwauk. From Nashwauk take State Highway 65 north to State Highway 1, then go west on Highway 1 for 10 miles.*

2. Belle Prairie County Park

Morrison County
(320) 632-0121
www.co.morrison.mn.us

This happened to be one of the first parks I visited when I began work on the guidebook because it was conveniently located on State Highway 371 north of Little Falls, along a route between the Twin Cities and northern Minnesota. I had seen the signs for Belle Prairie from the highway before, and it looked like nothing more than a nice wayside rest. Upon closer inspection, it turned out to be something special.

When entering the park, visitors are greeted by a large, dense stand of stately oak trees. The entrance road was actually laid out around some of the larger trees. After driving through the oak forest, visitors then catch a glimpse of the Mississippi River. (There are about twelve county parks located on the Mississippi River in Minnesota, and they are all special.)

At Belle Prairie, canoes and small boats can be launched and landed, and fishing from shore is possible. Several types of fish can be found in the river. Within site of the river, the park's picnic area sits under the shade of large white pines, in stark contrast to the hardwoods at the park entrance. These pines are reminiscent of days gone by in northern Minnesota, when they once dominated the landscape. On the way out of the park, visitors pass by a moderate-sized prairie area representative of the landscape that once dominated the southwestern part of the state. All of these scenic wonders—the oaks, the Mississippi River, the white pines, and the prairie—are Minnesota in microcosm, and they can be viewed on one short drive through the park. Of course, the entire experience is much more enjoyable if people are a little more leisurely about their visit.

For a picnic or break from traveling, a shelter, picnic tables, playground equipment, and vault toilets are provided in the park. Short walking trails are also available.

Directions: From Little Falls, take State Highway 371 for 3 miles north to the park.

3. Bunker Hills Regional Park

Anoka County
(763) 757-3920
www.anokacountyparks.com

In the Twin Cities metropolitan region, Bunker Hills is a great regional park to visit in the northern half of the area, and Lebanon Hills (see p. 13) is its equal in the southern half of the area. Bunker Hills has something for everyone and, like Lebanon Hills, it is conveniently located close to a variety of urban attractions. Best of all, the many activities, resources, and facilities provided in the park are enough to keep even the most active person or family busy for at least a couple of days. Although located in suburban Coon Rapids, it offers a quiet and secluded country setting.

For starters, I recommend trying out the nearly 7.50 miles of trails in the park. Many use the trails for in-line skating, biking, and walking, and the trails are also groomed for cross-country skiing in the winter. Horseback riders, and even those who want to give horseback riding a try, can utilize one of the best stables in the area; it provides guided trail rides, group activities, and sleigh rides. As its name implies, Bunker Hills has a rolling terrain, which is dotted with a mixed hardwood forest and patches of open prairie.

For those who enjoy golf or water-related activities, Bunker Hills has something for them too. The Bunker Beach Water Park includes a wave pool, waterslides, an adventure pool, and a creative sand-play area that are sure to keep families entertained. Golfers can enjoy 18 holes of quality golf for all ability levels. A large picnic area and an archery range are also available.

I recommend making a reservation to stay in the campground. Both RV and tent campers are nicely accommodated. The tent camping sites are quiet and secluded; and, in keeping with the high standards of regional park facilities, the restrooms and showers are clean, efficient, and warm. The RV sites are also secluded and comfortable. From the campground, visitors can easily and quickly access the park's myriad of things to do and see.

Directions: *From Anoka, take State Highway 242 east for 4 miles; the park entrance is on the left side of the road. A vehicle permit is required in the park.*

4. Chester Woods Park

Olmsted County
(507) 285-7050
www.olmstedpublicworks.com

T he rugged bluff country of southeastern Minnesota features numerous rivers and streams but not many lakes. Perhaps this is what makes Chester Woods special. As part of a larger flood control project for the nearby city of Rochester, this park, dam, and reservoir were completed in 1994 at the headwaters of Bear Creek. The great features of this park include more than one thousand acres of mixed hardwood forest, remnants of native prairie grasses, and several visitor-friendly and handicap-accessible recreation facilities.

At over one hundred acres in size, Chester Lake provides a variety of water-related activities for park visitors. Boaters can rent a canoe or launch their own canoe or small boat. Since park regulations restrict motorboats to only those powered by electric motors, boating here is a quiet experience. With a fishing rod and some bait, one can pursue largemouth bass, pan fish, or catfish from the waters. On a hot summer day, the large sandy beach will provide some cool relief. For those who prefer to fish from shore, there are four fishing piers provided at various locations. Two of the piers are handicap-accessible.

The developed campground and picnic area are also well designed and accommodate a variety of visitors. Tent or RV camping is available among the wooded sites. The modern restrooms and showers are clean and handicap-accessible. Seven different shelters provide a quiet and enjoyable picnic experience for those who can only stop by for the day.

For more adventurous souls who want to get out on the trails, Chester Woods can also accommodate a variety of needs. A 1-mile-long paved trail connects the

Chester Woods Park

picnic area, campground, and fishing facilities. Hikers will enjoy the 15 miles of trails that loop through the hardwood forest, prairie openings, and along Chester Lake. Along the trails, whitetail deer and wild turkeys are plentiful, as well as several species of songbirds. Horseback riders can enjoy more than 8 miles of park trails if trail conditions are favorable. When a blanket of snow falls on the park, skiers can experience winter in the hardwood forest along 8 miles of trail groomed for cross-country skiing.

Directions: Chester Woods is located 7 miles east of Rochester on U.S. Highway 14.

5. Collinwood Regional Park

Wright County
(320) 286-2801
www.co.wright.mn.us

With over ten thousand lakes, Minnesota has a tremendous freshwater resource. Collinwood Regional Park is located on one of those resources, Collinwood Lake, which sits on the Wright and Meeker County Line. The park and the lake are symbolic of the need to preserve such ecological treasures. The need is becoming greater every year, because private development along the state's shorelines has been growing exponentially over the past two decades.

Collinwood Lake and Collinwood Regional Park illustrate how natural shorelines provide fish and wildlife habitat, reduce storm water runoff, and maintain scenic and peaceful settings for outdoor enjoyment. Here, the proof of the pudding is that the lake, more than 500 acres in size, supports a variety of fish, including pan fish, northern pike, and walleye. Anglers can hook fish from their boats, and those who don't have a boat can walk out on the floating fishing pier, cast a line, and wait for a bite. Recreational boating is also popular here.

Campers can expect to find a comfortable campground with several shaded sites, clean restrooms, and warm showers. A short walk down the hill leads visitors to the beach, creative playground, and picnic area. With over 300 acres of land, hikers and skiers can utilize the park's 5 miles of trails that weave through the mixed hardwood forest and open meadows.

Directions: *From Buffalo, take State Highway 25 south for 8 miles, then turn right and go west on U.S. Highway 12 for 19 miles to Rhoades Avenue, which is 3 miles west of Cokato. Turn south on Rhoades and drive 2 miles to 70th Street SW, where the campground is located.*

6. Dunton Locks County Park

Becker County
(218) 847-0099
www.co.becker.mn.us

In this park, located in the lakes area of southern Becker County, visitors are greeted by a mixed hardwood forest of oaks, elms, and maples. The landscape primarily consists of forested and rolling hills in addition to shoreline on the two lakes.

Most of the park facilities are conveniently located near each other, offering visitors the opportunity to have a picnic or walk the lakeshore all in the same area. For those who want to hike or mountain bike, the park's terrain can be explored from several miles of trails.

At first glance, Dunton Locks looks like any other lakeside park, with the requisite facilities, including a beautiful trail system. What makes the park special, however, is the history of the small stream connecting Muskrat Lake and Lake Sallie. Interpretive panels alongside the trail tell the story.

From 1890 to 1918 this location featured water locks that would allow steamboats to travel among the area's chain of lakes. In fact, there were several locks built on numerous lakes in the Detroit Lakes region, which was booming with resorts and summer homes around 1900. Small steamboats provided easier access than the rough and narrow road system.

Today the locks are long gone, and Becker County has worked cooperatively with the Department of Natural Resources to establish a set of rock rapids between the lakes. Visitors now can stand on the bridge that crosses the stream and imagine steamboats filled with passengers passing through on their way to resorts and cabins. Recreational boaters can still travel between Muskrat Lake and Lake Sallie, now with the assistance of a small tramway operated on weekends by the county. Conveyances like this are not very common, so visitors may want to bring their boats, not only for the unique overland trip but also for the sheer beauty of plying the area's waters.

Directions: From Detroit Lakes, take U.S. Highway 59 south for 2 miles; turn right and go 0.30 mile on County Road 6. Then turn left and go 1 mile south on County Road 19. The park is located to the east of the DNR Fish Hatchery.

7. Elm Creek Park Reserve

Three Rivers Park District
(763) 694-7894
www.threeriversparkdistrict.com

T he large park reserves and regional parks around the Minneapolis and Saint Paul metropolitan area serve an important and lasting purpose. They preserve natural landscapes and provide a variety of outdoor recreation opportunities. All of these things are true at the Elm Creek Park Reserve in northern Hennepin County. The park's close proximity to a large portion of the urban population makes it a premier recreation destination and ecologically important area.

Connecting people with nature is part of the park district's mission, and at Elm Creek, the Eastman Nature Center supports that effort. It provides displays, wildlife viewing, interpretive trails, and a qualified staff. For example, visitors can learn about bird and mammal behavior, explore the wonders of a wetland, or see how animals survive in the winter.

With 80 percent of the park reserve protected in its natural condition and nearly 20 miles of trail in the park, there are many opportunities for solitude. Whether they bring their boots, a horse, or a bicycle, visitors can leave behind urban sprawl and shopping malls to become immersed in the park's natural world. The park also features several picnic areas and a man-made swimming pond that is a popular summer destination.

The park will not disappoint winter enthusiasts either. It features a downhill ski area, sledding hill, tubing hill, and 5 miles of ski trails. They all have lights for evening use, and all but half of the ski trails feature snowmaking equipment. So when the temperature is cold enough but the snow doesn't fall, people still ski or use the hill areas.

All in all, I can't think of a better way to keep people connected to nature and refreshed in their physical and mental health than a visit to Elm Creek.

Directions: From the western edge of the Twin Cities metro area, take U.S. Highway 169 north for 6 miles to State Highway 81; then turn left and take State Highway 81 northwest for 3 miles to Territorial Road. Take Territorial Road to the park entrances.

8. Gale Woods Farm

Three Rivers Park District
(952) 472-9203
www.galewoodsfarm.com

Some people tend to forget that large areas of Minnesota are composed of rich farmland that has produced crops and livestock for generations of consumers around the world. So it is not surprising that a county-run facility is dedicated solely to a celebration of this heritage. What is surprising, however, is that the agriculturally themed facility is located in Hennepin County, on the west side of the sprawling Twin Cities area.

Gale Woods Farm is a working, educational farm designed to provide experiences that foster understanding about agriculture, food production, and land stewardship. When visitors drive into the farm, the first thing they notice is the large red barn that houses sheep, cattle, chickens, and other livestock. Visitors will also observe several acres of land that is cultivated as orchards, gardens, and small crop fields using sustainable farming methods.

The Gale family, which had owned the farm for generations, donated the land for this unique park in 2000. It was their desire that it serve as a place where people could gain a deeper understanding of farm life. In addition to the agricultural experience, the facility also offers 3 miles of trails for hiking, biking, snowshoeing, or cross-country skiing. Visitors can also access Whitetail Lake by using the fishing pier or carry-in canoe access; or they can have a picnic in the large picnic area. Large groups or special events can reserve the "red barn" pavilion that seats up to 400 people.

While most parks are centered on nature and outdoor activities, Gale Woods Farm offers even more by presenting a complete farm experience. Farm education for adults and youth in particular is becoming more and more important as our society becomes more urbanized and people lose sight of the fact that much of our food still originates on farms.

The park district staff maintains a schedule of programs throughout the year at the farm, and special programs for groups can be scheduled in advance. It is best for people to call ahead of time to see what programs are scheduled or to schedule their own.

Directions: From Plymouth, take Interstate 494 south for 3 miles, then take U.S. Highway 12 west for 13 miles to County Road 92; turn left and go south for 9 miles, then take County Road 110 east for 3 miles.

9. Garvin Park

Lyon County
(507) 532-8214
www.lyonco.org

Over seven hundred acres of forest, valleys, and streams are preserved in this park. It is a refuge for a wide variety of birds, animals, and plants not often found across the wide-open expanse of southwestern Minnesota. This stretch of the Cottonwood River features several oaks, elms, and a variety of other trees, plants, and wildlife, all set within a picturesque valley that provides some much-needed topographic relief.

Visitors are offered two campgrounds, several picnic areas, miles of trails, turkey and deer hunting seasons, and a kid-friendly winter tubing hill. One of the campgrounds is designed to accommodate campers and their horses. The network of trails includes opportunities for hiking, horseback riding, and cross-country skiing.

Garvin represents the best of citizen involvement in protecting park areas

View from the observation tower at Garvin Park.

and establishing county parks. Elected officials and local citizens, with the help of Winona businessman H. C. Garvin, originally established this area as a park in 1935. It was used quite a bit for the next few years, but spring flood damage and lack of use left it quietly abandoned until 1967. Then local citizens and elected officials once again took action to acquire additional acreage and re-construct recreational facilities.

During my several visits, I was excited and a bit overwhelmed by the park's numerous valleys and the many opportunities for hiking and camping. The most memorable visit included a short hike to the observation platform near the north campground. From a treetop vantage point, visitors can enjoy views of the forest and valley. I couldn't help but think about what the view is like in the fall when the leaves are changing color. Winter is also an exciting season to visit, with the tubing hill and miles of ski trails.

Directions: *From Marshall, take U.S. Highway 59 south for 13 miles.*

10. Hole in the Mountain County Park

Lincoln County
(507) 368-9350
www.co.lincoln.mn.us/Departments/Parks.htm

L ocated on the edge of the town of Lake Benton, the park features over 800 acres of hardwood forest and steep terrain at the base of the Buffalo Ridge. In this corner of southwestern Minnesota, the flat terrain goes on for miles. But travelers approaching Lake Benton will be greeted by the sight of Buffalo Ridge rising above the prairie and an adjacent valley. The ridge, part of a glacial moraine formed thousands of years ago, has been measured as the windiest location in Minnesota and one of the windiest in the Midwest. Winds sweeping off the Great Plains are so powerful that energy companies have installed large wind generators on the ridge to take advantage of this renewable resource.

Within the park, several miles of hiking and horseback-riding trails take visitors through steep terrain under the cover of oaks, elms, and ash trees. The trails lead to several small historical sites. If visitors want to picnic or just relax, they can enjoy a quiet afternoon under the shade of oaks in the valley or on the ridge.

The park also features a small campground at the base of the ski hill. Modern restrooms are found in the chalet building. Electrical hookups, tables, and fire rings are provided. A separate horse-camping area is located across the road.

During the winter, the park is transformed into a downhill ski area. Although the slopes are rated from beginner to intermediate levels, and a towrope is the only way to the top, the area provides the only downhill skiing for miles around. Plus, the fee is modest.

A combination of the unusual terrain—at least for southwestern Minnesota—the abundant hardwood forest, and the downhill skiing makes Hole in the Mountain a unique and special place.

Directions: *From Marshall, take State Highway 23 southwest for 20 miles. Then take U.S. Highway 14 west for 13 miles to the park.*

11. Kensington Runestone County Park

Douglas County
(320) 763-6001
www.co.douglas.mn.us

R olling hills, prairie grasses, small ponds, and a mixed hardwood forest are highlights of this historic park. The site is the former farmstead of Olaf Ohman, which has been allowed to return to a natural prairie and forest condition.

The landscape at Kensington Runestone County Park has been restored to natural prairie and forest.

A large barn-style pavilion is available for large group picnics, and several picnicking areas are provided in a couple of locations throughout the park. The best way to experience the landscape of the park is from one of the several hiking /cross-country skiing trails that wind their way through the stands of trees, around pothole lakes, and to the top of prairie knolls.

The Ohman farmstead holds a place in history, because in 1898 Olaf Ohman discovered the Kensington Runestone while clearing trees on his farmstead. According to the inscriptions, the stone is believed to have been left by Viking explorers during the fourteenth century. Almost immediately the authenticity of the stone was questioned. How or why would Viking explorers be in central Minnesota in the fourteenth century? However, numerous scholars have studied the stone and determined that it was real. The debate regarding the authenticity of the stone has continued ever since it was unearthed in that quiet farm field. Over the years, scholars and experts have continued to offer differing opinions about the stone.

Young children may not understand the Runestone story, but they should certainly enjoy the views from the picnic area and the playground equipment. What makes this park special is its connection to Minnesota's past and its natural landscape. People can connect with this history by visiting the monument in the picnic area that marks the general location of the Runestone's discovery. Several displays in the park also interpret the history of the stone. In nearby Alexandria, the actual stone is on display at the Kensington Runestone Museum.

Directions: *From Alexandria, take State Highway 27 west for 14 miles, then take County Road 103 south for 1 mile; the park entrance is on the left side of the road.*

12. Lebanon Hills Regional Park

Dakota County
(952) 891-7000
www.co.dakota.mn.us/parks

L ebanon Hills is a perfect example of an urban regional park. Located in the cities of Apple Valley and Eagan, it is within easy driving distance to several metropolitan attractions such as the Mall of America and the Minnesota Zoo. For those looking for a quiet camping experience, but who still want to visit some of the city attractions, Lebanon Hills is one of the best places to visit. For local residents, the park also provides a variety of outdoor recreational and nature opportunities within a short distance from home.

The best place to begin a visit is at the park's visitor center. Built in 2003, it was designed and constructed using sustainable building standards. This was done to further enhance the environmental education mission of the Dakota County Park System and Lebanon Hills Regional Park. The location of the building was carefully considered in order to minimize ecological impacts, preserve green space, maximize energy efficiency (which includes growing grass on the roof), and treat stormwater runoff in an environmentally friendly manner. Educational programs, visitor services, and equipment rental are operated from the center. On hot summer days, the beach next to the visitor center on Schultz Lake provides some cool relief.

The enormous variety of activities available here is mirrored in the many roads leading into the park, and no one road is considered as the facility's main artery. Once inside, visitors have their pick of things to do. For horse lovers who don't own a horse, the Diamond T Ranch located in the middle of the park operates a stable with a regular schedule of trail rides and lessons. The park offers nearly 10 miles of horse trails. Rental and trail ride fees vary.

Mountain bike enthusiasts have their own network of trails on the far-western edge of the park, with over 4 miles of loops that present various degrees of difficulty. Hiking and canoeing enthusiasts will not be disappointed in what they find. Over 13 miles of hiking trails traverse the rolling hills and forested landscape. Paddlers can avail themselves of a 2-mile-long canoe trail on several small lakes, with four portages providing access to the heart of the park.

A regional park wouldn't be complete without a properly equipped campground, and Lebanon Hills is no exception. Campers will find a neat, clean, and quiet campground for both RV and tent camping. My experience of tent camping in the more secluded sites was great. Although the RV campground is a little more crowded, the feeling of being miles away from a major urban area persists. Clean, efficient, and warm restrooms and showers also make the camping experience enjoyable. Lebanon Hills is a great place to camp or to enjoy the outdoors in a setting readily accessible to urban dwellers.

Directions: From Minneapolis, take Cedar Avenue south to Cliff Road (County Road 32) in Eagan, then go east on Cliff Road. The mountain bike trailhead and park campground are south on Johnny Cake Road; the Diamond T Ranch and Jensen Lake are south on Pilot Knob Road; and Holland Lake is adjacent to Highway 32. To get to the park's visitor center and beach, follow the Schulze Lake signs.

13. Long Lake Park and Campground

Clearwater County
(218) 657-2275 (summer)
(218) 694-6227 (winter)
www.longlakepark.com

Long Lake Park and Campground offers a friendly and welcoming atmosphere to enjoy camping and outdoor recreation. The landscape includes a mixed forest of birch, aspen, spruce, and young red pines. Another notable feature of this park is its location on the Mississippi River/Hudson Bay Watershed Continental Divide. While not as dramatic or famous as the Continental Divide along the Rocky Mountains, this one separates water that flows to the Mississippi River and the Gulf of Mexico on one side and to Hudson Bay and the North Atlantic on the other. A watershed is a significant topographical feature, and it's fun to contemplate the long distances and the different directions of water flows. This fun and educational activity benefits everyone who values and treasures the importance of protecting water, one of

A surprising variety of playground equipment can be found in county parks

Minnesota's valuable natural resources. The topography here is not dramatic, but it does include rolling hills.

The heart of the park is a well-planned campground. Loop roads feature an ideal range of sites for accommodating tents, pop-up campers, and RVs of various sizes. A picnic area, fishing dock, boat ramp, and short hiking trail are also provided. Also, Long Lake is 80 feet deep and spring-fed, which creates crystal-clear waters that are perfect for boating, trout fishing, or scuba diving. With a 10 mph speed limit on the lake, it is an ideal place to paddle a canoe or kayak, and scuba-diving groups are regularly seen using the lake.

Everything that people enjoy about a park can be found here: a comfortable campground, shoreline and boat fishing, the opportunity to enjoy boating on the lake, a sandy beach, and additional nearby destinations. One of them, Itasca State Park, is only minutes away. These amenities offer everyone in the family something for entertainment.

Directions: From Bagley, take State Highway 92 south for 13 miles, then turn left on State Highway 200 and go east for 3 miles.

14. Mound Creek County Park

Brown County
(507) 233-6640
www.co.brown.mn.us

Mound Creek County Park preserves a part of the unique bedrock landscape that is characteristic of the southwestern Minnesota prairie. At Mound Creek, the bedrock is visible as a waterfall formation near the picnic area and the south end of the lake. Visitors can follow a short trail from the picnic area or a parking lot to the waterfall. During dry periods, the waterfall is nothing but a trickle of water, but it is still illustrative of the area's geology. Just a few miles away, in Cottonwood County, are two other geologically interesting sites: the Jeffers Petroglyphs Historic Site, located just to the south, and Red Rock Falls Park (described elsewhere in this section), which lies immediately to the west.

The terrain of the park is indicative of the large expanse of prairie that once dominated the landscape of southwestern and western Minnesota, as well as the Great Plains. Primarily devoid of trees, the prairie was considered by early settlers as a desert, but they soon discovered that the soil was rich with nutrients and began the process of tilling and planting farm fields. This transformation meant the loss of wildflowers, plants, and animal habitat, as well as increased soil erosion. Several county parks in the western and central regions of Minnesota contain preserved prairies or have restored former prairies in order to mitigate some of the lost terrain.

Mound Creek contains more than 300 acres of rolling prairie with open views of the 70-acre reservoir the park surrounds. Visitors can get a profound appreciation for prairie life just by walking about and listening to the wind blow through the park's tallgrass expanses. Anglers can fish the lake, but they should be aware of the special catch and release regulations that are in effect here. The lake can also provide relief on hot days with a visit to the small beach located downhill from the picnic area. Picnickers have a choice of one of many tables or the shelter. The park also features 3 miles of hiking trails and a nine-hole Frisbee-disc golf course.

Directions: From New Ulm, take U.S. Highway 14 west for 36 miles to the junction with U.S. Highway 71, turn left and go south on Highway 71 for 9 miles, turn left and go east on County Road 10 for 2 miles, then turn left and go north on 450th Ave.

15. Phelps Mill County Park

Otter Tail County
(218) 998-8470
www.co.ottertail.mn.us/phelpsmill/

I n the late 1800s, local settlers determined that a section of the Otter Tail River, near what was to become the little village of Phelps, was a perfect location for a flourmill. Here, the river offered a steep elevation drop and fast-moving water, two things needed to turn machinery.

Phelps Mill began operation in 1889 and was an immediate success. The residual effects spurred a general store, other businesses in Phelps, and new roads. At the turn of the century, rural flour milling in Minnesota was bustling, with a readily available and abundant source of wheat in the fields nearby and a steady demand for flour. Gradually, transportation routes and processing costs for flour forced most small mills out of business, one by one. The Phelps Mill changed hands a few times as others tried to make it work, but in 1939 it stopped milling and closed down. The mill stood abandoned until the 1960s, when local residents championed the idea of preserving it. In 1965 Otter Tail County purchased the

Restored flourmill at Phelps Mill County Park.

mill and designated it as a county park. In 1975 the Phelps Mill was given the honor of being placed on the National Register of Historic Places.

The great thing is that even in bad weather visitors will find something to pique their interest. Inside the mill, there are exhibits and authentic machinery that tell the story of how flour was milled in days gone by. A short walk across the dam offers views of the mill and the picnic area below. This park provides a history lesson for those who are willing to take the time to stop for a while and explore its features. Local residents also continue to celebrate their past with the annual Phelps Mill Festival held every July.

A large picnic area with shelters is provided for visitors to the park. The primary attraction, however, is the mill.

Directions: From Fergus Fall, take County Road 27 north for 5 miles, then County Road 10 east for 4 miles; the road then turns into County Road 1. Continue east on it for 7.5 miles, following the park signs.

16. Plum Creek Park

Redwood County
(507) 859-2491
www.walnutgrove.org

This park encompasses more than 200 acres of land along Plum Creek and includes the area where the creek is held back by a large earthen dam to form Lake Laura. Large hardwood trees and a few pines cover the landscape.

The park actually has two developed areas. The main picnic area contains trails, shelters, and several ball fields, all located in the creek valley. The campground and swimming beach are located to the west of the picnic area. The swimming beach is secluded, and the small reservoir lake keeps boat traffic to a minimum.

The park is noteworthy because the childhood home of author Laura Ingalls Wilder is located only a couple of miles away, on Plum Creek. In a series of books about the frontier, Wilder wrote about this area and others in the Midwest; and television made them popular with the Little House on the Prairie series. Kids and adults both can imagine the young Wilder sitting on the banks of Plum Creek as she soaked up images and impressions that would find expression in her writing. If she were around today, she would be surprised to see the modern facilities found in the picnic area and campground

Visitors will enjoy the park because of its quiet setting, its wealth of activity options, and because of the nearby historical attractions. By taking the time to hike a trail or camp overnight, visitors are sure to have a positive experience and enjoy a unique historical area.

The actual Ingalls homestead is located only a short drive from the park, and the Laura Ingalls Wilder Museum is located in the nearby city of Walnut Grove.

Every July, local residents celebrate this history by performing the Wilder Pageant, an outdoor drama depicting Laura's years at Plum Creek.

Directions: From Redwood Falls take U.S. Highway 71 south for 19 miles, then take U.S. Highway 14 west for 16 miles to Walnut Grove. Take County Road 14 west for 1 mile, and then take County Road 78 south for another mile.

17. Quarry Park and Nature Preserve

Stearns County
(320) 255-6172
www.co.stearns.mn.us/departments/parks

Quarry Park and Nature Preserve is located on the edge of Saint Cloud and features a landscape of trees, wetlands, and water-filled quarries. A large section is protected as a Scientific and Natural Area, which contains a significant example of a natural community of plants and wildlife in a granite bedrock landscape. This natural habitat is a haven for animals and birds on the edge of an urban area.

The combination of history and natural beauty makes Quarry Park unique.

A large parking lot provides plenty of room for visitors who come to use the network of hiking and mountain-biking trails, to swim or fish in designated ponds, or to catch a glimpse of birds, animals, or plants. Picnic areas, a dock for swimming access, an observation platform, and a new rock-climbing area are also provided.

Quarry Park is a unique combination of history and natural beauty that is well worth a visit. Around 1900, Saint Cloud red granite was discovered and subsequently quarried from this land. The stone was used in buildings like the Saint Paul Post Office and the James J. Hill House. Quarry operations ceased in the 1950s, and the land began to heal. Since the 1950s nature has been allowed to reestablish itself in the park. In 1992 Stearns County began acquisition of the park, which today totals over 600 acres.

A quiet fog hung in the air on the summer morning that I visited, when I nearly had the park to myself. After a brisk hike down the trail, I quickly came upon the first of several former quarries that have been filled with water to form crystal-clear ponds. Some of these ponds are 200 to 300 feet deep. To get the most out of the park, visitors should be sure to hike the trails and stop to take a look at the quarry ponds. Their mirror-smooth water provides a great photo op.

The combination of history and natural beauty make this a unique county park. It represents the ability of nature to restore a landscape back to its natural wonder and the ability of humans to recognize environmental restoration as valuable for both ecological and recreational benefits.

Directions: *From Saint Cloud take State Highway 23 west, turn left on 10th Avenue and then go south to the first stop sign; turn right and go west on County Road 137 for almost a mile. A vehicle permit fee is charged for entry into the park.*

18. Rapidan Dam Park

Blue Earth County
(507) 625-3281
www.co.blue-earth.mn.us

Rapidan Dam Park features a beautiful setting along the Blue Earth River downstream of the Rapidan Dam. This stretch of river features a largely undisturbed landscape that features the "Big Woods" hardwood forest unique to southern Minnesota. High rock bluffs and side streams can also be found along this stretch.

The Rapidan Dam store serves as the park office and is also famous for its pies, so visitors should make a point to stop in and try a piece. The park was recently redeveloped, changing from drive-in campsites to primitive hike-in-only campsites located along the river. This unique campground offers a quiet retreat for those willing to hike a short distance and set up a tent. One campsite at the end of the park road is designed as handicap-accessible. Except for some hike-in group camps, this is the only county park in Minnesota that features a hike-in-only campground.

Another reason to enjoy this great hiking park is its namesake dam, which visitors can walk across while enjoying a beautiful view of the river valley below. Only the canoe access is visible downstream.

The fishing and canoeing opportunities are enough to sustain even the most dedicated anglers or paddlers. A parking area and canoe launch provide access for anyone who seeks an adventurous paddle down the river. Several kinds of fish can be found in the river. The scenery on view is spectacular.

Directions: From Mankato, take U.S. Highway 169 south for 10 miles, then turn left and go east on County Road 9 for 1.5 miles.

19. Red Rock Falls Park

Cottonwood County
(507) 831-2060
www.rrcnet.org~cotton/cotpark.html

This is a small park with a special feature: a formation of red rock dells and a waterfall along Mound Creek, all hidden from view by a cover of mixed hardwood trees. The brilliant green of the trees and shrubs provides a fine setting for the exposed, deep-red bedrock and a shimmering green pool of water. Although Red Rock Falls and the dells are only around 30 feet high, they are a beautiful sight not often found in southwestern Minnesota.

A parking lot and mowed trails are the only maintained facilities on site. Vault toilets, a picnic area, and playground equipment are not maintained. This minor drawback, however, is quickly forgotten after visitors see Red Rock Falls.

Most first-time visitors pulling into the parking lot are unaware that such unique formations are close at hand. In fact, there are no directions or signs leading to the dells to indicate that this place is special. The only clues are the sound of falling water and the mowed trails leading to the creek. But it doesn't

Red rock dells are hidden among the trees at Red Rock Falls County Park.

take long to discover the park's hidden treasures and view the gently falling water.

Although small in comparison to other parks, Red Rock Falls represents one of the benefits of county parks: the protection of unique local historical or natural areas. The park's outcropping of bedrock and dells formations along Mound Creek are a rare sight in Minnesota. We're lucky that all this has been preserved as a park. ***Directions:*** *From Windom, take U.S. Highway 71 north for 17 miles, then turn right and take 250th Street east for a half mile.*

20. Rice Creek Chain of Lakes Regional Park Reserve

Anoka County
(763) 757-3920
www.anokacountyparks.com

For those longing for the gentle swoosh of a paddle alongside a canoe or the thrill of seeing wildlife in natural habitats, this park should be on a must-see list. With seven lakes within its boundaries, a canoe is the best way to explore the Rice Creek Chain of Lakes Regional Park Reserve. Four of the lakes are part of the designated canoe trail, so I recommend launching at one of them, George Watch Lake, for a day of paddling and portaging through the park. Paddlers should remember to bring lunch, plenty of water, a camera, a map, and a sense of adventure. They will paddle along scenic and natural shorelines, hear the wind blowing through the leaves, see birds take flight, and maybe catch a glimpse of a deer that has come down to the water for a drink. For those without their own craft, the park rents canoes and kayaks at the Wargo Nature Center, which also offers canoeing and kayaking classes in the summer.

As a 6-mile-long stretch of lakes, wetlands, and forest located in the northern suburbs of the Twin Cities metropolitan area, Rice Creek Chain of Lakes is an important tract of natural habitat. It is home to a variety of wildlife and plant species, including a large blue heron colony located at Peltier Island on Peltier Lake. At the Wargo Nature Center, visitors can learn about the blue heron and many other wildlife species that make this place their home. The nature center serves as the hub of education and natural discovery within the park. Children and adults alike can enjoy learning about and connecting with the outdoor environment through organized programs.

In addition to providing valuable wildlife habitat and a quiet canoeing or kayaking experience, the park also offers a variety of other outdoor recreational opportunities. Visitors will find that the modern campground accommodates tent and RV campers and includes clean, modern restrooms with showers. A sandy swimming beach and picnic area are located on Centerville Lake. The picnic area includes a reservation-only pavilion, tables, and grills. Peltier and Centerville lakes are popular fishing locations, and in the middle of the park sits the scenic 18-hole Chomonix Golf Course for those craving a little action on the links. There are also 4 miles of nature trails near the nature center and 4 miles of paved trails that weave through the park. The paved trails connect to the regional trail system in Lino Lakes.

Directions: *Rice Creek Chain of Lakes Regional Park Reserve is just east of Interstate 35W in the Lino Lakes area. The Wargo Nature Center is located just off County Road 14.*

21. Rum River North County Park

Anoka County
(763) 757-3920
www.anokacountyparks.com

Rivers have sparked the imagination and have been a focus of human endeavor since time immemorial, so it is pleasant to note that rivers are a central feature of many Minnesota county and regional parks. The Rum River is one such highlight, rivaled, in my mind, only by the Mississippi for its beauty and power. Managed as a Wild and Scenic River by the Minnesota Department of Natural Resources, the Rum offers many opportunities for adventure and discovery. Three parks run by the Anoka County Park System along the river contribute to this experience. And Rum River North County Park, the northernmost of the three, is one of my all-time Minnesota favorites.

Here visitors will find a thick forest of hardwood trees hugging a riverbank, combined with upper oak woodlands and restored prairie areas. Paved hiking and biking trails offer connections between the picnic areas and the river access. The picnic pavilions are perfect for large groups, and a year-round building that houses meeting rooms is a good place to hold a gathering close to the beautiful outdoors.

With a short carry-in access, this park is the perfect place to begin a day or overnight trip on the river. Like the other two parks along the river administered by Anoka County, Rum River North features canoe campsites for those looking for a backcountry camping experience during their paddle. The park also features a handicap-accessible fishing deck that allows people of all abilities the opportunity to feel the tug of a fish on the line and the battle that ensues. Walleye, northern pike, and smallmouth bass have been known to populate the river. Rum River North, as well as its two sister parks, are ideal launching spots for a canoeing or kayaking trip sure to please even the most jaded paddlers.

Directions: From Anoka, take County Road 9 north for 13 miles to County Road 24; turn left and go west for a half mile, then turn right on County Road 72 and drive one block to the entrance.

22. Saint Croix Bluffs Regional Park

Washington County
(651) 430-8240
www.co.washington.mn.us

The name of this park conjures up images of ravines and high rock cliffs along the Saint Croix River valley. When one drives through the park, however, most of this signature terrain is nowhere to be found, with the campground and picnic area located on flat ground that rises above the river valley. It is only when visitors get on a hiking trail or drive down to the boat landing that they see the steep slopes and ravines, all shielded by a dense forest of mixed hardwoods, spruce, and pines. With this varied landscape, there are great opportunities for spotting eagles, turkeys, or grouse.

The enchanting river bluff landscape is further enhanced by the facilities provided within the park. Campers will enjoy the large campground that features several campsites and clean restrooms. Around 5 miles of hiking and cross-country skiing trails will keep even the most avid hiker or skier busy. In addition, if boaters are itching to get their craft into the water, a small harbor and double concrete ramps provide easy access to the Saint Croix River, which has long been a popular destination for fishing and boating. It has been used as a vital waterway from the very beginnings of human habitation in the area. Recognizing its historical and scenic value, the federal government designated the entire Saint Croix as a National Wild and Scenic River in 1972.

The park's Conference Cottage and Group Camp provide opportunities for small and large groups to come and enjoy the park. A large picnic area with several shelters, modern playground equipment, athletic fields, and restrooms offers enough space to accommodate even the largest group picnics. With such a wide variety of activities, both land- and water-based, it's easy to see why the park is one of my favorites, an opinion shared by a lot of other fans of Minnesota's parks. *Directions: From Stillwater, take County Road 21 south for 16 miles.*

23. Sandy Point County Park

Jackson County
(507) 847-2240
www.co.jackson.mn.us

Sandy Point County Park was established in the same way that a majority of Minnesota's county parks were created—with funding from the federal Land and Water Conservation Fund. This program, administered through the state, has provided numerous counties with the funding to purchase and develop parks since the 1960s. Jackson County used this source of funding in 1971 to help purchase Sandy Point County Park, located on South Heron Lake.

The 8,000-acre South Heron Lake, North Heron Lake, and surrounding prairie and wetland habitats are recognized as one of the best waterfowl production areas in the state by the Department of Natural Resources. In fact, nineteenth-century accounts of this area tell about the abundance of waterfowl on the two Heron lakes. In the late 1800s, hunters recognized the need for conservation regulations to prevent overexploitation of the birds. The same is still true today, as state regulations have designated North and South Heron lakes as Waterfowl Feeding and Resting Areas. As such, during the hunting season, restrictions limit the use of motorboats only to those with electric trolling motors of 30 pounds of thrust or less, and even these can only operate in designated parts of the lakes.

During a visit to Sandy Point, visitors can climb to the top of the observation tower or find a spot to sit along the sandy shoreline to look out across Heron Lake and view plentiful numbers of birds, particularly ducks, geese, or white pelicans. Even if no birds are spotted from the observation tower, the view is still gorgeous.

Park facilities also include a picnic shelter, tables, grills, playground equipment, ball fields, and vault toilets. Campers can bring their RV or tent and set up in the small campground. I recommend that they get up early in the morning to watch for birds. It is only a short walk to the observation tower from the campsites, and the sunrise alone is worth the effort.

Directions: From Jackson, take Interstate 90 west for 9 miles, then State Highway 86 north for 3 miles. Turn left on County Road 20 and go 3.50 miles west to the park.

24. Spring Lake Park Reserve

Dakota County
(952) 891-7000
www.co.dakota.mn.us/parks

Awe-inspiring scenery awaits visitors to Spring Lake Park Reserve, where rugged bluffs and scenic views of the wide and majestic Mississippi River valley are abundant. Onlookers can observe how the mighty river begins to carve a large and winding path as it continues on its journey to the Gulf of Mexico.

With high river bluffs and steep ravines, this park is a haven for a wide variety of wildlife. It's not uncommon to spot soaring eagles, swooping hawks, deer or rabbits darting along the trail.

Each season plays a unique role in shaping the beauty of this park. In spring, the hard dry grass turns to green and the bare branches fill with leaves. During the summer, visitors can challenge themselves to see how many wildflowers they can identify or they can relax in the shade of the hardwood trees. The fall brings the glorious change of colors and crisp breezes. Winter offers snow for cross-country skiing and snowshoeing activities.

For those seeking a quiet stroll, 4 miles of trails are available. There is a nice picnic area, with two shelters, several tables, and modern restrooms. Children can enjoy a large play structure or the open playfields. One open field is specifically designated for flying model airplanes.

The western side of the park features a unique outdoor archery range with practice targets and two walking loops with targets. Permits are required for the archery trail, as well as for the model airplane field.

Directions: *Spring Lake is located 14 miles east of Apple Valley on County Road 42.*

25. Three Island Lake County Park

Beltrami County
(218) 759-4210
www.co.beltrami.mn.us

A thick forest of mixed hardwoods, spruce, and pines fills the landscape of this natural area park. The scenic Turtle River, Three Island Lake, and surrounding forest create a serene atmosphere. The effect is particularly enhanced during autumn, when the forest is in full color, or winter, when a thick blanket of snow muffles all but a few forest sounds.

Quiet and unassuming, this park has been kept in a natural condition with only minimal development of access roads, parking lots, and trails. The trail system accommodates hiking, mountain biking, horseback riding, and cross-country skiing; a short stretch has been set aside for snowmobiling. A small dirt boat ramp provides access to the lake.

This park and I go way back. While I was a student at Bemidji State University, it was the first county park I ever visited. I vividly recall taking family members out on the trails with skis and snowshoes and enjoying the winter wonderland of snow, ice, and running water of the Turtle River. My past experiences with the solitude and beauty of skiing on the trails here make the park one of my favorites for the winter season and one of my favorite parks anywhere, anytime.

Directions: *From Bemidji, take U.S. Highway 71 north for 11 miles, then turn left and go west on County Road 23 for 2.5 miles; watch for the county park sign.*

SOME FAVORITE PARKS *for Special Uses*

Family Camping

My young family and I camp whenever we get the chance, so I know that family camping is full of unique challenges and outstanding rewards. There is no better way to teach children about the outdoors and to spend quality time together than packing up the camping gear and heading for a park.

The needs of families on a camping venture are as varied as the parks themselves. Whether a family uses an RV/camper or a tent, there are some common elements that campgrounds should have in order to provide an enjoyable experience. These parks should have clean and comfortable restrooms/toilets, a friendly campground atmosphere, and enough activities to keep the kids busy. Usually, trails and water-related activities of some kind are also important to meet these needs. The following parks are some of the best for family camping.

Schroeder Regional Park on Cedar Lake in Wright County has all the park activities located within easy walking distance from the campground. This makes it easy to keep an eye on the kids and for them to stay busy. It features 50 campsites, a large creative play structure, a large sand beach, a fishing pier, and modern restrooms with showers.

County Park 7 in Kandiyohi County has a similar-sized campground and swimming beach on Games Lake. It also features a park store with a small arcade and is located near Sibley State Park, which features additional trail and nature activities.

Oxbow Park in Olmsted County has trails, a nature center with regular programs, and a small zoo that features a variety of animals.

Daly Park in southern Blue Earth County includes volleyball and tennis courts, modern play structures, a beach, several locations for fishing, and a natural island that can be explored. Another nice feature is that the tent-camping areas are separate from the RV campsites.

Baylor Regional Park in Carver County offers nice campsites, clean facilities, a large beach, and open playfields.

Bunker Hills Regional Park in Anoka County and **Lebanon Hills Regional Park** in Dakota County both have comfortable campgrounds and offer a variety of family-friendly activities.

For those looking for a remote family camping experience—fishing and swimming activities that are likely to satisfy the kids—then **Bass Lake County Park** in Itasca County is an excellent choice.

With the largest campground of all county parks, **Baker Park Reserve** in Hennepin County has plenty of family activities. Located on Lake Independence on the west side of the metropolitan area, the park is convenient to other attractions (such as movie theaters) if the weather turns bad. Over 7 miles of paved bicycle trails are enough to wear out even a teenager. Water-related activities include a large beach, fishing piers, and paddleboat/rowboat/kayak/ canoe rentals. The park is kept safe through the use of strong campground regulations and regular patrols by park district police. In addition, the Baker Near-Wilderness Settlement is a group facility that holds year-round programs or can be rented by families. Rustic cabins and amenities offer families a chance to leave the phone and television at home.

Historical Sites

Historical sites offer an opportunity to look into the past. Exploring these areas can be fun and educational for adults and children.

The Three Rivers Park District celebrates Minnesota's history from the mid- to late 1800s at **Historic Murphy's Landing** in Scott County. Visitors can walk among historical buildings and meet costumed characters who depict life during this pioneer era. It can be a substantial learning experience, so schools and groups commonly schedule trips to Murphy's Landing. The facility is open on weekends throughout the year.

The days when the railroad dominated transportation in the United States are celebrated at **End-O-Line Railroad Park** in Murray County. Beginning with local volunteers and a historic railroad turntable, this facility has added several buildings, equipment, and memorabilia over the years. Historic buildings include a country schoolhouse, general store, railroad foreman's house, water tower, gristmill, engine house, and restored depot. Among the railroad equipment is a red caboose, diesel switcher, and steam locomotive. A visitor center, picnic area, and restrooms also make this a great place to stop for a couple of hours.

End-O-Line Railroad Park preserves the heritage of the locomotive era.

The park is open during the summer from Memorial Day through Labor Day.

Manomin County Park in Anoka County features the Banfill-Locke Tavern. Originally built in 1847, it is on the National Register of Historic Places. This park also offers picnic facilities and scenic views of the Mississippi River.

Anoka County Riverfront Regional Park preserves the Riedel Farm originally established in the 1880s. The farmhouse has been restored and is available for group rentals. A picnic area is also provided.

Kensington Runestone County Park in Douglas County is the location where the famous runestone was discovered in 1898.

Phelps Mill County Park in Ottertail County preserves the history of Minnesota's small rural flourmills.

(More details about these last two parks can be found in the "25 Favorite County Parks" section of this guide.)

Horseback Riding

There are several county parks that feature extensive and well-groomed trails open to horseback riding. Facilities, mileage, conditions, and seasons for riding vary at each location. For those people with their own horses, these parks are great destinations. For those without horses but not without the urge to saddle up, there are two regional parks in the metropolitan area with stables that offer guided trail rides and other horse programs.

Garvin Park in Lyon County features 5 miles of horse trails. A horse staging area and parking lot is provided next to the southern campground. Riders will be delighted by the park's varied terrain and scenic landscape of mixed hardwoods.

Dassel/Darwin County Park in Meeker County offers a few miles of horse trails. A scenic overlook and picnic area is located in the wayside rest area of the park.

Crow-Hassan Park Reserve in Hennepin County provides 9 miles of horse trails during the summer and 1.5 miles during the winter. A large parking area, hitching posts, and a water pump are provided. For those who want to camp, a group camp can be reserved in advance.

The Three Rivers Park District also offers horse trails in the **Murphy-Hanrehan Park Reserve** located in Scott County. Nearly 10 miles of summer trails and 3 miles of winter trail are provided. A group camp can also be reserved for camping.

Skalbekken County Park in Renville County features a beautiful Minnesota River valley riding experience. A small campground with vault toilets is provided

Horse trails wind through Skalbekken County Park.

within the thick, river-valley hardwood forest. Several miles of horse trails can be explored.

Lake Elmo Park Reserve in Washington County is very friendly for horse campers. It includes a campground loop specifically designated for campers with horses and has water, portable toilets, and 20 campsites. Horseback riders can explore 8 miles of horse trails through the park's rolling hills of forest and prairie.

Hole in the Mountain County Park in Lincoln County accommodates horse campers and offers 5 miles of horse trails. Around 800 acres of hilly woodlands and prairie can be experienced.

Bunker Hills Regional Park in Anoka County features 4 miles of horse trails and the Bunker Park Stables, which offers trail rides and other programs. (Details about this park can be found in the "25 Favorite County Parks" section of this guide.)

Lebanon Hills Regional Park in Dakota County allows horseback riding on 10 miles of trail. The Diamond T Ranch, located in the middle of the park, offers trail rides and other various services.

Nature Centers

For many people, their best connection to the outdoors or nature is through organized activities. Nature centers focus on providing these activities in a fun and educational atmosphere. Children and adults can both learn a lot by participating in nature hikes, watching for wildlife, studying wetland ecology, or learning how to identify different plant and tree species. A large part of the future in understanding conservation and natural resources rests in the educational purpose and focus of nature centers.

The **Tamarack Nature Center** is located on three hundred acres of the Bald Eagle–Otter Lakes Regional Park in Ramsey County. It offers a variety of community and school programs focused on understanding, appreciating, and enjoying the natural world. Forests, prairies, wetlands, and Tamarack Lake are home to a wide variety of plants and animals.

The **Lowry Nature Center**, located on the Carver Park Reserve in Carver County, features programs like pond studies, stargazing, and birding for children, adults, and families. Several trails traverse forest, marsh, meadow, and tamarack swamp landscapes in order to foster wildlife observation. Lowry also features a very unique outdoor education play structure called "Habitats," where children can explore larger-than-life plant and animal habitats.

The **Joseph E. Wargo Nature Center**, situated on the Rice Creek Chain of Lakes Regional Park Reserve in Anoka County, includes a large facility with classrooms, meeting room space, and outdoor equipment rental. School and family programs on topics such as winter survival and wildlife observation are designed to foster an appreciation of the responsibility and relationship we have with the environment. Wildlife can easily be viewed from inside the nature center or along one of its hiking trails.

The **Eastman Nature Center**, on the Elm Creek Park Reserve in Hennepin County, provides exhibit areas, displays, and hands-on learning activities under one roof. Outside, 4 miles of nature trails lead nature lovers through a forest, over a pond, near a creek, and past a prairie area. Opportunities for viewing wildlife are common. The nature center holds regular programs and can schedule programs for groups.

Inside the **Richardson Nature Center**, a classroom and exhibits support the outdoor and environmental education mission of the Three Rivers Park District. The center is located on the Hyland Lake Park Reserve in Hennepin County. Four nature trails can be followed that explore forest, water, wetland, and prairie landscapes. Programs and activities change with the seasons—for example, snow-shoeing in winter, watching for birds in spring, exploring life in a pond in summer, and making apple cider in fall.

Picnicking

Picnicking is the most common activity found in Minnesota's county and regional parks. As a result, just about every park has some sort of picnic area, with anywhere from one picnic table to over a hundred tables. Having a picnic is probably the easiest way to enjoy any of the state's parks, from the most scenic and expansive to the plainest and most commonplace.

Ramsey County boasts three parks with topnotch picnicking possibilities. **Vadnais–Snail Lakes Regional Park** features a large picnic pavilion overlooking Snail Lake and the swimming beach. For those looking for a quiet, one-table picnic experience, the nearby hill has tables spread throughout. Modern restrooms and a large play structure are also provided. **Island Lake County Park** features three reservation-only shelters, numerous tables, a large play structure, a fishing pier, and modern restrooms. **White Bear Lake County Park**, in addition to having one of the top beaches, features a nice grassy and open picnic area with tables and grills.

Point Douglas Park in Washington County is located at a beautiful location where the Saint Croix River forms a lake before flowing into the Mississippi River. Tables and restrooms are provided.

Clearwater/Pleasant Regional Park in Wright County is a popular picnic site with several tables, a reservation-only shelter, and modern restrooms.

Lake George Regional Park in Anoka County has seven shelters, numerous tables and grills, play structures, and modern restrooms.

Swimming

When the Minnesota summers get hot and humid, our favorite destinations are lakes and rivers. The state's county parks are rife with quality swimming areas. For me, a top-quality swimming beach features nice sand, comfortable and clean facilities, and easy access. In recent years, several counties have had to limit the number of lifeguards they can put on their beaches. Remember to swim cautiously and to supervise young children at all times.

Le Homme Dieu Beach in Douglas County features a long stretch of sand and a modern bathhouse. During the summer, lifeguards are on duty in the afternoons when the air temperature reaches 68 degrees or warmer.

Each of Kandiyohi County's county parks has beaches, but **County Park 4** in Spicer is one of the best. Fine sand and the warm waters of Green Lake greet visitors to this park. Lifeguards are on duty during the summer.

Several of the regional parks in the Twin Cities metropolitan area have built swimming ponds to accommodate the demand for swim areas. **Lake Minnetonka Regional Park** in Hennepin County features one of these man-made ponds. Designed with a sandy shoreline and bottom, they feature a constant depth and a filtration system that keeps the water safe and sanitary. A modern bathhouse is provided and lifeguards are on duty regularly.

Lake George Regional Park in Anoka County has a beautiful beach with clear water, several picnic pavilions, and a quiet natural setting. A creative play structure and sand volleyball courts are also provided.

White Bear Lake County Park is a popular beach in Ramsey County. It includes a modern bathhouse, creative play structures near the beach, and a large picnic area. Lifeguards are on duty during the summer.

Square Lake County Park in Washington County is a beautiful setting, offering close to a thousand feet of sandy beach on a very clear lake. Lifeguards are on duty during the summer months, and a clean, modern bathhouse is provided.

Beebe Lake Regional Park and **Clearwater/Pleasant Regional Park** in Wright County each feature comfortable beaches and clean, modern restrooms.

Winter Recreation

Several parks remain open during the winter to provide trails and facilities for winter recreation, including cross-country skiing, snowshoeing, and downhill skiing or tubing. Winter in Minnesota can be a wonderful experience if people arm themselves with the proper clothing, equipment, and attitude. Propelling oneself on skis across the snow through cold, dry air or skiing down a snow-covered slope on a bright sunny day are both exciting and enjoyable winter activities. In addition, anyone can strap on a pair of snowshoes and take a walk through the snow-covered woods.

Hole in the Mountain County Park in Lincoln County is the only county park outside of the Three Rivers Park District that offers downhill skiing. Beginner- to intermediate-level skiing is provided, and a handle-and-rope lift and rental equipment are available.

Garvin Park in Lyon County has offered winter family fun on its tubing hill for years. Two-and-a-half miles of cross-country ski trails are also maintained.

Hyland Lake Park Reserve in Hennepin County features a complete downhill ski and snowboard area, a ski jump, and cross-country ski trails (4 miles of the trails are lighted).

For those seeking a northern Minnesota cross-country ski getaway, Beltrami County's **Three Island Lake County Park** and **Movil Maze Recreational Area** offer several miles of ski trails ranging from easy to difficult.

Washington County's **Saint Croix Bluffs Regional Park** features quiet cross-country skiing through fields and forest overlooking the river valley. Six miles of ski trails are groomed for traditional "in-line" skiing.

At **Bunker Hills Regional Park** in Anoka County, cross-country ski rentals, 20 miles of groomed trails, and 12 miles of skijoring trails are available, and the area is convenient to Twin City residents. Skijoring (skiing while harnessed to a dog) is becoming more popular, and regional parks are beginning to add trails for this winter use.

Dakota County's **Lebanon Hills Regional Park** is a wonderful winter retreat, featuring 20 miles of ski trails and 10 miles of trails open for snowshoeing.

When it comes to winter activities, **Elm Creek Park Reserve** in Hennepin County has everything. It features 18 miles of cross-country ski trails, a downhill ski area, a sledding hill, and a tubing hill. The tubing hill, downhill ski area, sledding hill, and 2.5 miles of ski trails can be covered by snowmaking machines. This feature ensures that snow will be on the ground when the temperatures are low enough. In order to provide recreational opportunities past sunset during the winter, the downhill ski area, tubing hill, sledding hill, and 5 miles of ski trails are lighted.

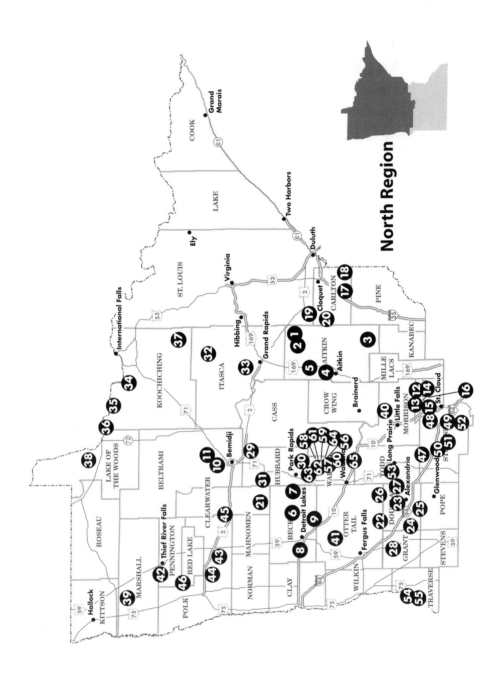

North Region

COOK

• Grand Marais

LAKE

• Two Harbors

ST. LOUIS

• Ely

• Virginia

• International Falls

• Duluth

PINE

⑱

⑰

CARLTON

• Cloquet

⑲

⑳

KANABEC

KOOCHICHING

㊲

ITASCA

• Hibbing

• Grand Rapids

㉑

AITKIN

• Aitkin

③

㉜

㉝

⑤

④

MILLE LACS

㉞

㉟

CROW WING

• Brainerd

⑬⑫⑭

• St Cloud

⑯

㊱

CASS

• Bemidji

㊶ Little Falls

MORRISON

⑮

⑱⑮⑮⑲

㊳

LAKE OF THE WOODS

BELTRAMI

⑪

⑩

HUBBARD

㉙

Park Rapids

㊽ Long Prairie

TODD

⑤⑧⑥⑥⑨

Wadena

㉟①㉚㊷

STEARNS

ROSEAU

CLEARWATER

㊺

②①

㉛

⑦ Detroit Lakes

⑨

OTTER TAIL

Fergus Falls

DOUGLAS

Alexandria

• Glenwood

㉔⑨

㊹ Thief River Falls

PENNINGTON

RED LAKE

MAHNOMEN

BECK

⑧

⑨

⑤①

POPE

KITTSON

• Hallock

MARSHALL

㊴

POLK

NORMAN

CLAY

WILKIN

GRANT

㉘

STEVENS

TRAVERSE

㊴⑤

40

GUIDE
TO COUNTY PARKS

NORTH REGION

Aitkin County

Land Department
209 2nd Street NW, Room 206
Aitkin, MN 56431
(218) 927-7364
www.co.aitkin.mn.us

1. Jacobson Campground

Quiet camping on the Mississippi River is provided at this small county campground. Visitors can enjoy water activities on the river or access to the nearby public forests.

Camping: There are 10 RV/tent sites provided, and each has a picnic table and fire ring. An artesian well provides drinking water and vault toilets are also provided. A fee is charged for overnight camping.

Picnic Area: None.

Water Recreation: A boat ramp provides access to the Mississippi River for boating and fishing.

Trails: None.

Recreational Facilities: None.

Seasons: The campground is open from May 1 through October 15.

Directions: From Aitkin take U.S. Highway 169 north to Hill City; then from Hill City, take State Highway 200 east to Jacobson. The campground is located one mile northwest of Jacobson on the west side of the Mississippi River.

2. Jacobson Wayside Rest

This wayside rest is located on the Mississippi River and offers travelers a nice break along their journey. Hardwood trees provide shade as one gazes at the park's scenic landscape.

Camping: None.

Picnic Area: The wayside rest features several picnic tables and grills. Vault toilets are also provided.

Water Recreation: None.

Trails: None.

Recreational Facilities: None.

Seasons: The wayside is open from May 1 through October 15.

Directions: From Aitkin take U.S. Highway 169 north to Hill City; then from Hill City, take State Highway 200 east to Jacobson. The wayside is located on the left-hand side of the road just before the Jacobson Bridge.

3. Snake River Campground

This campground provides a nice location for hunters, trail users, and river users who want to camp in southern Aitkin County. Features include primitive camp-sites and toilet facilities.

Camping: There are 12 RV/tent sites provided, and each has a picnic table and fire ring. Vault toilets and a water pump are also provided. A fee is charged for overnight camping.

Picnic Area: None.

Water Recreation: A carry-in canoe access is provided to the Snake River.

Trails: The campground is connected to Aitkin County's Redtop and Soo Line All Terrain Vehicle (ATV) trails, which provide several miles of ATV riding opportunities.

Recreational Facilities: None.

Seasons: The campground is open from May 1 through October 15.

Directions: From Aitkin take State Highway 47 south for 28 miles, then State Highway 18 east for 12 miles, and finally State Highway 65 south for 3 miles; watch for the campground sign.

4. Aitkin Campground

Located on the Mississippi River, this campground offers convenient camping close to town. The river at Aitkin is small and quiet but still provides enjoyable boating and fishing opportunities.

Camping: Features include seven RV/tent sites located on the shore of the river. Each site has a picnic table, fire ring, and electrical hookups. There are vault toilets, a water pump, and an RV dump station. A fee is charged for overnight camping.

Picnic Area: None.

Water Recreation: A small concrete boat ramp provides access for small motorboats and/or canoes to the river.

Trails: None.

Recreational Facilities: None.

Seasons: The campground is open from May 1 through October 15.

Directions: In Aitkin, from State Highway 210, take 4th Avenue NW north for one quarter mile.

5. Berglund Park

Set along the meandering shore of the Mississippi River in Palisade, this park offers scenic picnicking and convenient camping facilities. Visitors can also enjoy fishing and relaxation along the riverbanks.

Camping: There are nine RV/tent sites. Each includes a picnic table, campfire ring, and electrical hookups. Vault toilets and a water pump are also provided. A fee is charged for overnight camping.

Picnic Area: Several picnic tables and a shelter are provided.

Water Recreation: A small concrete boat ramp provides access for small motorboats and/or canoes to the river. Benches and a handicap-accessible fishing pier are located on the riverbank.

Trails: The Soo Line recreational trail can be accessed from the park.

Recreational Facilities: None.

Seasons: The park is open from May 1 through October 15.

Directions: From Aitkin take U.S. Highway 169 north to the junction with County Road 3, then take County Road 3 east to Palisade; the park is located in Palisade next to the bridge.

Becker County

Natural Resources Management
PO Box 787
200 E. State Street
Detroit Lakes, MN 56502
(218) 847-0099

6. Chilton Park

Chilton Park is a small public access located in eastern Becker County.

Camping: None.

Picnic Area: None.

Water Recreation: A concrete ramp provides motorized and nonmotorized boat access to Bass Lake.

Trails: None.

Recreational Facilities: None.

Seasons: The park is open year-round.

Directions: From Detroit Lakes go east on State Highway 34 for 18 miles, then turn left and go 1 mile north on County Road 39; the park is on the left side of the road.

7. Clauson Park

Clauson Park is a small public access located in eastern Becker County. It is relatively undeveloped and features a thick canopy of trees.

Camping: None.

Picnic Area: None.

Water Recreation: A small carry-in trail provides canoe access to Knutson Lake.

Trails: None.

Recreational Facilities: None.

Seasons: The park is open year-round.

Directions: From Detroit Lakes go east on State Highway 34 for 26 miles, then turn right and go 4 miles south on County Road 47; turn left and drive 4.25 miles east on County Road 42, then turn right onto Knutson Lake Drive; go a third of a mile to the park.

8. Dunton Locks County Park

Dunton Locks offers a combination of scenic beauty and historical significance. From 1890 to 1918, nine steamboats occupied the waters of Muskrat Lake and Lake Sallie, and the Dunton Locks allowed each boat passage between the lakes. Today the locks are gone, but a short marine railway continues to transport boats between the lakes.

Camping: None.

Picnic Area: A modern shelter complete with kitchen, restrooms, and numerous tables make this park a nice place for large gatherings.

Dunton Locks County Park

Water Recreation: Shoreline fishing is possible. A nearby concrete ramp allows motorized and nonmotorized boat access to Lake Sallie.

Trails: There are approximately 8 miles of hiking, mountain biking, and cross-country ski trails that wind through a mixed deciduous forest of oaks, maples, and elms. In addition, a paved bicycle/hiking trail connects the park to Detroit Lakes.

Recreational Facilities: None.

Seasons: The park is open year-round.

Directions: From Detroit Lakes, take U.S. Highway 59 south for 2 miles; turn right and go a third of a mile on County Road 6. Then turn left and go 1 mile south on County Road 19. The park is located to the east of the DNR Fish Hatchery. (*To read more about the park, see "25 Favorite County Parks" in the first section of this guide.*)

9. Lions Park

This small day-use park is cooperatively managed with the Lion's Club of Frazee. It is a popular location for family gatherings during the summer.

Camping: None.

Picnic Area: One large modern shelter with a kitchen facility and a second smaller shelter provide plenty of room for picnic groups. The larger shelter also includes restrooms.

Water Recreation: None.

Trails: None.

Recreational Facilities: Older playground equipment is provided.

Seasons: The park is open from April through October.

Directions: From Detroit Lakes take U.S. Highway 10 south for 7 miles to Frazee, then turn left and go north a third of a mile on County Road 29. Watch for the large turkey on the right side of the road that marks the entrance to the park.

Beltrami County

Natural Resource Management Department
505 Bemidji Avenue, Suite 3
Bemidji, MN 56601
(218) 759-4210
www.co.beltrami.mn.us

10. Movil Maze Recreational Area

Movil Maze features an extensive network of multiple use trails on over 1,000 acres of forestland. It is a very popular destination for mountain biking and cross-country skiing.

Camping: None.

Picnic Area: None.

Water Recreation: None.

Trails: There are several miles of nonmotorized, multiple-use trails that can be used for hiking, mountain biking, and cross-country skiing. In addition, a segment of a snowmobile trail runs through the area.

Recreational Facilities: None.

Seasons: The park is open year-round for day use.

Directions: From the junction of U.S. Highways 2 and 71 in Bemidji, drive north on 71 for 7 miles to Wildwood Road; then turn left on Wildwood Road and go north for a half mile to the parking area.

11. Three Island Lake County Park

Three Island Lake County Park features an extensive network of nonmotorized, multiple-use trails within a beautiful forest setting. The best times to visit this park are fall and winter—vibrant colors of a mixed hardwood forest light up the park in the fall, and snow blankets the trails that wind along the Turtle River in the winter.

Camping: None.

Picnic Area: An open area near the old dam can be used for picnicking. No facilities are provided.

Water Recreation: The Turtle River is very scenic and the rushing water offers a soothing sound. The park features a dirt boat ramp that provides access for boating, fishing, canoeing, or kayaking on the waters of Three Island Lake.

Trails: Several miles of nonmotorized, multiple-use trails can be used for hiking, mountain biking, horseback riding, and cross-country skiing. In addition, a segment of a snowmobile trail runs through the park.

Recreational Facilities: None.

Seasons: The park is open year-round for day use.

Directions: From the junction of U.S. Highways 2 and 71 in Bemidji, drive north on Highway 71 for 11 miles to County Road 23; turn left (west) on 23 and drive 2.5 miles, watching for the County Park sign. Turn left onto Three

Island Road NE and go 1 mile to the main parking lot. The boat ramp and an undeveloped picnic area are further up this road.
(To read more about the park, see "25 Favorite County Parks" in the first section of this guide.)

Benton County

Parks Department
531 Dewey Street
PO Box 129
Foley MN, 56329
(320) 968-5035
www.co.benton.mn.us

12. Benton Beach

With a large sand beach, picnic area, and campground, Benton Beach provides a variety of opportunities for day and overnight visitors alike. A unique feature of this park is the Lakeview Conference Center located on the lakeshore. The center includes a meeting room and a large open deck on the water's edge, available for group and special event rentals.

Camping: Several campsites are located in the park. Each site has a stone fire ring and some include electrical hookups. A shower/restroom building is provided for the campground and adjacent picnic area. The park also provides an RV dump station. A fee is charged for overnight camping.

Picnic Area: The picnic area includes one small picnic shelter, two large picnic shelters, and numerous tables. Restrooms and a handicap-accessible portable toilet are located adjacent to the picnic area. A fee is charged for picnic shelter use.

Water Recreation: A large sandy beach provides enjoyable swimming access to Little Rock Lake. A dirt boat ramp is also provided for motorboat, canoe, or kayak access.

Trails: None.

Recreational Facilities: A large modern playground, older-style playground equipment, two sand volleyball courts, a small baseball field, and horseshoe pits are provided.

Seasons: The park is open year-round. The campground is open from May through September.

Directions: From Saint Cloud, go north on U.S. Highway 10 to Rice (watch for the Benton Beach sign). At the stoplight on Highway 10 in Rice, turn east on County Road 2 and go 2.5 miles to the park entrance, which is on the right side of the road.

13. Graves Farm County Park

The Graves Farm is the most recent addition to the Benton County Park System. This regional park features 3,300 feet of undeveloped Mississippi River shoreline and 289 acres of native prairie and hardwood forest areas. Future development plans include two parking areas, a picnic area, a playground, and the development of nonmotorized trails.

Camping: None.

Picnic Area: None.

Water Recreation: Scenic views of the Mississippi River can be found from walking trails within the park. Steep slopes and the protection of slope vegetation prevent water access.

Trails: None. Conceptual plans for the park include designation of several hiking trails throughout the park property. These trails were not designated or signed at the time this guidebook was written.

Recreational Facilities: None.

Seasons: The park is open year-round.

Directions: From Saint Cloud, go north on U.S. Highway 10 to Rice; at the stoplight in Rice, turn left (west) on County Road 2 and go through town, then take a left turn onto County Road 55 just after crossing the railroad tracks. The park is located 1.5 miles south of Rice on County Road 55.

14. Mayhew Lake County Park

Located on the south end of Mayhew Lake, this small day-use park features picnicking and fishing opportunities. Several large oak trees frame the landscape and provide a beautiful setting for any visitor to enjoy.

Camping: None.

Picnic Area: A picnic table, grills, and seasonal portable toilets are provided.

Water Recreation: A concrete boat ramp is provided at the park for access to Mayhew Lake.

Trails: None.

Recreational Facilities: None.

Seasons: This park is open year-round.

Directions: From Saint Cloud, go north on U.S. Highway 10 to County Road 13, then turn right (east) and take 13 to the little town of Mayhew; turn right (south) on County Road 1 and go 1 mile, then turn left (east) onto County Road 43. The park is on the left side of the road after about 1 mile.

15. Rose Anna Beach

Rose Anna Beach is a small park located on the southwest side of Little Rock Lake. This park is not currently developed with any facilities. It is primarily used to provide winter access to the lake.

Camping: None.

Picnic Area: None.

Water Recreation: There is access from the shoreline to fish at Little Rock Lake.

Trails: None.

Recreational Facilities: None.

Seasons: The park is open year-round.

Directions: From Saint Cloud, go north on U.S. Highway 10 to Rice (watch for the Benton Beach sign); at the stoplight in Rice turn east on County Road 2 and go 1.5 miles to West Lake Road, then south on West Lake Road for 2.5miles. The park is on the left side of the road.

16. Saint Regis Park

Saint Regis Park is a small day-use park located on the west side of Little Rock Lake. It preserves a small piece of lakeshore for public use during both the summer and winter seasons.

Camping: None.

Picnic Area: A level lawn all the way to the lake includes a few picnic tables and grills for visitor use. A seasonal handicap-accessible portable toilet is provided.

Water Recreation: Shoreline fishing on Little Rock Lake is available.

Trails: None.

Recreational Facilities: None.

Seasons: The park is open year-round.

Directions: From Saint Cloud, go north on U.S. Highway 10 to Rice (watch for the Benton Beach sign); at the stoplight in Rice, turn east on County Road 2 and go 1.5 miles to West Lake Road, then south on West Lake Road for 2 miles. The park is on the left side of the road.

Carlton County

Building Maintenance Department
301 Walnut Avenue
Carlton, MN 55718
(218) 384-9100
www.co.carlton.mn.us

17. Bear Lake County Park

Situated on the wooded shoreline of Bear Lake, this park features 120 acres of parkland for camping, picnicking, and swimming. It is easily accessible from Interstate 35 near Barnum.

Camping: A small campground features several RV sites and three tent sites, all located along the lake. Restrooms and showers are also provided. A fee is charged for overnight camping, and a caretaker lives on-site.

Picnic Area: There are basic facilities for picnicking, including a few tables and grills.

Water Recreation: Bear Lake offers swimming, fishing, and boating opportunities. A beach and boat access is provided.

Trails: A few short hiking trails are provided.

Recreational Facilities: A small playground is located near the campground.

Seasons: The park is open from May through September.

Directions: From Cloquet, take Interstate 35 south for 14 miles to the Barnum exit; turn left, then right onto the frontage road and follow it to the park.

18. Chub Lake County Park

A large grassy picnic area is located on a small hill that overlooks Chub Lake, providing scenic vistas for visitors. The park also provides baseball fields for athletic events.

Camping: None.

Picnic Area: Facilities include a large shelter, picnic tables, grills, and vault toilets.

Water Recreation: Visitors can enjoy swimming, boating, and fishing opportunities at Chub Lake. A boat ramp, fishing dock, and swimming beach are provided.

Trails: None.

Recreational Facilities: Three baseball fields are located a short distance from the lake on the backside of the park.

Seasons: The park is open from May through October.

Directions: From Cloquet, take State Highway 45 south for 3 miles, then County Road 3 south for 1 mile to East Chub Lake Road; follow the park signs.

19. Island Lake County Park

Picnics and swimming on Island Lake can be enjoyed at this park, which is located in northwestern Carlton County. For those looking to camp, a private campground is conveniently located next to this park.

Camping: None.

Picnic Area: Facilities include a shelter, several picnic tables, and vault toilets.

Water Recreation: A sand beach provides swimming opportunities in Island Lake. Boats can be launched from a nearby public boat ramp.

Trails: None.

Recreational Facilities: None.

Seasons: The park is open from May through October.

Directions: From Cloquet, take State Highway 33 south for 1 mile, then Interstate 35 south for 2 miles to State Highway 210; go west for 18 miles, then take County Road 120 south for a half mile.

20. Kalavala County Park

This park is a small wayside rest area located near Kettle River. It is primarily used by travelers on Highway 73.

Camping: None.

Picnic Area: A few picnic tables and vault toilets are provided.

Water Recreation: None.

Trails: None.

Recreational Facilities: A baseball diamond is provided.

Seasons: The park is open year-round.

Directions: From Cloquet, take State Highway 33 south for 1 mile, then Interstate 35 south for 17 miles to the Moose Lake exit; take State Highway 73 west and north for 6 miles to Kettle River.

Cass County

There are no county parks in Cass County.

Clay County

There are no county parks in Clay County.

Clearwater County

Land and Forestry
213 Main Ave. N.
Bagley, MN 56621-8309
(218) 657-2275 (summer)
(218) 694-6227 (winter)
www.longlakepark.com

21. Long Lake Park and Campground

Long Lake Park and Campground is nestled within the gently rolling fields and forests of Clearwater County on the shores of beautiful Long Lake. It offers a family-friendly atmosphere for camping and outdoor enjoyment. Activities for children, accessible lake amenities, and a clean, comfortable campground are all provided on 53 acres of parkland.

Camping: The campground features 90 RV/tent sites, two handicap-accessible sites, vault toilets, an RV dump station, and handicap-accessible restrooms with showers. A fee for camping is charged, and reservations are accepted. A camp store offers a variety of snacks and small supplies for campers.

Picnic Area: Picnic tables and grills are provided near the boat access and fishing pier. A shelter is also available for rental.

Water Recreation: The crystal clear waters of Long Lake make it a popular destination for scuba diving. With a 10 mph speed limit, the lake is ideal for fishing, canoeing, kayaking, or paddleboating. A concrete boat ramp, swimming beach, and handicap-accessible fishing pier are provided for lake access.

Trails: A 1-mile-long hiking trail is provided. There are also several forest trails in the area that offer mountain biking opportunities.

Recreational Facilities: Older-style playground equipment, volleyball courts, horseshoe pits, and basketball courts are provided.

Seasons: The campground is open from mid-May to mid-September, with primitive camping available during the fall hunting season.

Directions: From Bagley, take State Highway 92 south for 13 miles, then turn left on State Highway 200 and go east for 3 miles. The park entrance is on the right side of the road.

(To read more about the park, see "25 Favorite County Parks" in the first section of this guide.)

Cook County

There are no county parks in Cook County.

Crow Wing County

Parks Department
Complex West, 301 Laurel Street
Brainerd, MN 56401
(218) 824-1115
www.co.crow-wing.mn.us

Crow Wing County has some public water accesses, a few trails on county forest lands, and some land set aside for county parks. However, at the time of this book's publication the county did not have any developed county parks and was in the process of developing a comprehensive development plan for county parks and trails. For updates or additional information please contact the Parks Department.

Douglas County

Public Works Department
Parks Division
PO Box 398
Alexandria, MN 56308
(320) 763-6001
www.co.douglas.mn.us

22. Chippewa County Park

Chippewa County Park is located on 37 acres of land between Little Chippewa Lake and Devils Lake in central Douglas County. Visitors can enjoy scenic views of the lakes, a variety of recreational opportunities, and historical features that include evidence of early Native American settlement and the site of the first two county fairs.

Camping: A small campground is provided, with six RV sites and two tent sites. Facilities include picnic tables, fire rings, and a restroom/shower building. A fee is charged for overnight camping.

Picnic Area: The picnic area includes several picnic tables, grills, and fire rings. A large shelter is also available for picnic use and can be reserved by calling the Parks Division office.

Water Recreation: Fishing from the shore is a popular pastime, and shoreline runs along both lakes. A small sandy boat ramp on Little Chippewa Lake makes it possible to launch a canoe or small boat. The isthmus of land between the lakes provides a nice location for swimming on a hot summer day.

A picnic shelter looks out over Little Chippewa Lake at Chippewa County Park.

Trails: None.

Recreational Facilities: Horseshoe pits are provided near the campground.

Seasons: The park is open year-round. The campground is open from May through September.

Directions: From Alexandria, take County Road 82 northwest for 13 miles to Brandon, then take County Road 7 north 1 mile; turn left and take County Road 108 west 1 mile to the park entrance, which is on the right side of the road.

23. Deputy Sheriff Curtis A. Felt Memorial Park

This small day-use park was named in honor of a Douglas County law officer, who lost his life in 1978 in the line of duty. The park is conveniently located only minutes north of Alexandria, and is used frequently by residents of the county for picnics and group gatherings.

Camping: None.

Picnic Area: The picnic area includes numerous picnic tables, grills, and two shelters for group use. Water fountains and a handicap-accessible portable toilet are also provided. The shelters can be reserved by calling the Parks Division office.

Water Recreation: None.

Trails: None.

Recreational Facilities: Older-style playground equipment, some newer play structures, a campfire ring, a sand volleyball court, and a softball/baseball field are provided.

Seasons: The park is open from April through October.

Directions: From Alexandria, take County Road 42 north 1 mile; the park is on the right side of the road.

24. Kensington Runestone County Park

Encompassing 193 acres, this site is Douglas County's largest park and flagship destination. The park includes the Olaf Ohman farmstead and the 1898 discovery site of the Kensington Runestone. The Runestone is believed to have been left by Viking explorers in the early 1300s, yet the authenticity of its origins has been questioned over the years.

Camping: None.

Picnic Area: The picnic area includes several picnic tables, a campfire ring, and a shelter. A large, enclosed gathering hall designed like a red barn is available for group rentals. Restrooms are located in the red barn. A second picnic area is located further down the park road near the hill where the Kensington Runestone was discovered. Tables, a shelter, a water pump, and a handicap-accessible vault toilet are provided.

Water Recreation: There are a few small ponds and wetlands in this park.

Trails: A few miles of trails wind through the park property. The trails are mowed during the summer and groomed for cross-country skiing in the winter.

Recreational Facilities: Older-style playground equipment is provided near the main picnic area, along with a sand volleyball court, horseshoe pits, and a grassy open playfield.

Seasons: The park is open year-round.

Directions: From Alexandria, take State Highway 27 west for 14 miles, then take County Road 103 south 1 mile. The park entrance is on the left side of the road.

(To read more about the park, see "25 Favorite County Parks" in the first section of this guide.)

25. Lake Brophy County Park

This county park is a small wayside rest area that sits high on the shoreline over-looking Lake Brophy. Originally built as a wayside rest along old Highway 52, the park was transferred to the county, along with the road, when Interstate 94 was completed. The scenic picnic area makes this park a nice destination or wayside stop for visitors.

Camping: None.

Picnic Area: The picnic area features a handicap-accessible shelter, water pump, and several picnic tables. Vault toilets are also provided near the large parking lot. The picnic shelter can be reserved by calling the Parks Division office.

Water Recreation: A steep stairway provides walking access to the shoreline of Lake Brophy, which offers fishing and sightseeing.

Trails: None.

Recreational Facilities: The park provides older-style playground equipment, featuring swings and a slide.

Seasons: The park is open from April through October.

Directions: From Alexandria, take County Road 82 northwest 3.5 miles; the park is on the right side of the road.

26. Le Homme Dieu Beach

Le Homme Dieu Beach is a popular swimming location, featuring a nice sandy beach. It is located only minutes from Alexandria.

Camping: None.

Picnic Area: The beach includes several picnic tables for visitor use. In addition, the beach features newly remodeled handicap-accessible restrooms and a new parking lot.

Water Recreation: The swimming beach is open during the summer from noon to 7 p.m. daily, when the daytime temperature is 68 degrees or warmer. Lifeguards are on duty.

Trails: None.

Recreational Facilities: None.

Seasons: The beach is open during June, July, and August.

Directions: From Alexandria, take State Highway 29 north 2 miles; the beach is on the left side of the highway.

27. Spruce Hill County Park

Spruce Hill County Park is located in northeast Douglas County and includes the historical site of the Spruce Hill Pioneer Village. This park features 97 acres of forest, trails, and fields for visitors to enjoy.

Camping: None.

Picnic Area: The picnic area features numerous amenities, including several picnic tables, a handicap-accessible shelter, fire rings, a water pump, and vault toilets (including one handicap-accessible toilet). The shelter can be reserved by calling the Parks Division office.

Water Recreation: A small tributary of the Spruce Creek flows through the park. It is too small for any boating or fishing opportunities.

Trails: Four miles of cross-country ski trails wind through the park's forest. A snowmobile trail also passes through the park.

Recreational Facilities: Some open and grassy playfields and a developed softball field are provided.

Seasons: The park is open year-round.

Directions: From Alexandria, take State Highway 29 north 10 miles, then take County Road 5 east 5 miles to County Road 105 (a gravel road); take County Road 105 north a half mile to the park entrance, which is on the left side of the road.

Spruce Hill County Park

Grant County

County Courthouse
PO Box 1007
Elbow Lake, MN 56531
(218) 685-4520

28. Pine Ridge Park

Located on the shores of the Mustinka Flowage, Pine Ridge Park is home to an island of Norway pine trees, set amid farm fields. A unique feature of this park is the 1939 Works Progress Administration/DNR spillway dam that created the small lake.

Camping: None.

Picnic Area: The picnic area features numerous picnic tables and grills surrounded by red pines and large spruce trees. Other amenities include three shelters, several fire rings, and four vault toilets.

Water Recreation: The Mustinka Flowage offers visitors opportunities for

Pine Ridge Park offers access to the Mustinka Flowage.

fishing and small-boating. A dirt boat ramp is provided for canoes and small-boat launching. The park also features an unsupervised swimming beach with a swim dock and a nearby picnic shelter.

Trails: A short walking trail links the parking area to the spillway dam.

Recreational Facilities: Amenities include some older-style playground equipment and an open athletic playfield in the center of the park.

Seasons: The park is open year-round.

Directions: From Elbow Lake, take State Highway 54 south for 3.5 miles, then County Road 12 west for 7 miles to County Road 11; take County Road 11 south for 4 miles, then turn left and take County Road 34 east for a half mile to the park entrance, which is on the left side of the road.

Hubbard County

Parks and Recreation Department
101 Crocus Hill Street
Park Rapids, MN 56470
(218) 237-1456
www.co.hubbard.mn.us

29. Farris Park

Picnicking and outdoor enjoyment can be found at this day-use park in northeastern Hubbard County. A variety of facilities is sure to keep any family busy on a nice summer day.

Camping: None.

Picnic Area: The picnic area includes a shelter, picnic tables, and restrooms.

Water Recreation: None.

Trails: Facilities include a paved hiking trail.

Recreational Facilities: A basketball court, ball field, and tennis court are provided for visitor use.

Seasons: The park is open from May through September.

Directions: From Park Rapids, take U.S. Highway 71 north for 37 miles, then turn right and go east on County Road 9 for 5 miles.

30. Heartland Park

Located in the central section of Park Rapids, the park is very popular for swimming, trail access, and picnics. Large picnic facilities and easy access to the Heartland State Bicycle Trail make Heartland Park a popular recreation location.

Camping: None.

Picnic Area: Two shelters can be reserved for group picnics. Other amenities include picnic tables, grills, and handicap-accessible restrooms.

Water Recreation: A concrete ramp provides motorized and nonmotorized boat and fishing access to the Fish Hook River. The park also features a swimming beach.

Trails: A large parking lot provides plenty of space to park and access to the Heartland State Bicycle Trail. Maintained by the state DNR, this is a combination paved-and-gravel recreational trail that stretches from Park Rapids to Walker.

Recreational Facilities: Playground equipment, basketball courts, horseshoe

Bike or hike through the natural beauty of Heartland Park.

pits, and ball fields provide a variety of opportunities for visitors.

Seasons: The park is open from May through September.

Directions: The park is located in the middle of Park Rapids, approximately a half mile east of the intersection of State Highway 34 and U.S. Highway 71; then follow the sign from State Highway 34.

31. Lake George Community Park

The small community of Lake George takes pride in this local park. Visitors can enjoy lake access and picnic facilities beneath towering pine trees.

Camping: None.

Picnic Area: Two shelters, numerous picnic tables, and restrooms are provided.

Water Recreation: A dirt ramp provides motorized and nonmotorized boat and fishing access to Lake Paine. A swimming beach offers swimming opportunities.

Lake George Community Park offers lake access and recreational facilities.

Trails: None.

Recreational Facilities: A basketball court and ball field is provided for visitor use.

Seasons: The park is open from May through September.

Directions: From Park Rapids, take U.S. Highway 71 north and east for 23 miles to the tiny community of Lake George; the park is on the right side of the road just as you enter Lake George.

Itasca County

County Park System
1177 LaPrairie Avenue
Grand Rapids, MN 55744
(218) 327-2855
www.co.itasca.mn.us

32. Bass Lake County Park

Hidden in the northeast corner of Itasca County, Bass Lake County Park offers visitors an enchanting experience for camping, picnicking, fishing, and hiking in a near-wilderness setting. Majestic red and white pines flank the shoreline of the park's namesake lake, and trails weave through 663 acres of forest. The entire park gives a person an overall feeling of remoteness and solitude.

Camping: The campground features 29 RV/tent sites, water pumps, and vault toilets (including two handicap-accessible vault toilets). Each site has a picnic table and fire ring. An overnight fee is charged for camping. The campground's most attractive feature is that every campsite is located on the lakeshore.

Picnic Area: A medium-sized picnic area is located on the shore of Bass Lake with an open field and scattered red pines. Facilities include picnic tables, grills, a water pump, and vault toilets.

Water Recreation: Four small lakes provide fishing and swimming opportunities. Small, dirt boat ramps or carry-in public accesses are provided on each lake. All of the lakes can accommodate small motorboats. A swimming beach is located next to the campground.

Trails: There are several short loop trails that begin and end at various points along the roads in the park. They are open for multiple uses unless posted signs indicate closings.

Recreational Facilities: The park is also open to hunting during appropriate seasons. Rules and regulations prohibit hunting and loaded firearms within the campground and picnic area.

Seasons: The park and campground are open from early May through mid-October.

Directions: From Grand Rapids, take U.S. Highway 169 northeast to State Highway 65 at Nashwauk, then take 65 for 31 miles north to State Highway 1; go west on Highway 1 for 10 miles to the park entrance, which is on the left side of the road.

(To read more about the park, see "25 Favorite County Parks" in the first section of this guide.)

33. Gunn Park

Gunn Park is located on the shores of Prairie Lake only minutes north of Grand Rapids in central Itasca County. Originally developed as a model community park in 1956 by local paper company owner Charles K. Blandin, today this park serves as a scenic wayside rest along the edge of the Wilderness National Scenic Byway (State Highway 38). Its 45 acres are forever dedicated to public use as a county park.

Picnic tables nestle on the shore of Prairie Lake at Gunn Park.

Camping: None.

Picnic Area: Facilities include a large picnic area; a large, handicap-accessible, open-air pavilion; vault toilets; and a handicap-accessible portable toilet. The pavilion can be reserved for large groups. Numerous picnic tables and grills are provided.

Water Recreation: Prairie Lake offers fishing and boating opportunities. A concrete fishing pier is located in the park.

Trails: The 7-mile-long, paved Itasca Bicycle Trail connects Gunn Park to Grand Rapids. This trail also connects to the larger Mesabi Bicycle Trail, located only 3 miles south of the park.

Recreational Facilities: Older-style playground equipment and a volleyball court are provided. A baseball/softball field is also available for use on adjacent Itasca Little League property.

Seasons: The park is open daily from early May through early October.

Directions: From Grand Rapids, go 5 miles north on State Highway 38. The park entrance is on the right side of the road.

Kanabec County

There are no county parks in Kanabec County.

Kittson County

There are no county parks in Kittson County.

Koochiching County

Land and Forestry
715 4th Street
International Falls, MN 56649
(218) 283-1152
www.co.koochiching.mn.us

34. Loman Park

This park is a small day-use area located on the Black River in the small town of Loman. It is the former site of the town's general store from 1910 to 1965. It

The log cabin-style rest rooms at Loman Park are handicap-accessible.

was converted to a county park in 1965 and provides a nice spot to rest when traveling on Highway 11.

Camping: None.

Picnic Area: The picnic area includes several picnic tables, grills, a fire ring, an artesian well, and a nice, log-sided, handicap-accessible vault toilet.

Water Recreation: A small-boat ramp provides access to the Black River. From the Black River you can also access the Rainy River. Canoes or small boats are recommended.

Trails: None.

Recreational Facilities: None

Seasons: The park is open year-round.

Directions: From International Falls take State Highway 11 west for 23 miles to Loman. The park is on the right side of the highway in town.

35. Nelson Park

Located on the shore of the Rainy River, Nelson Park provides visitors with river access and camping facilities. It is most popular with people who pursue the Rainy River walleye.

Camping: The campground features six RV/tent sites and four primitive sites. The semideveloped sites include a table and a fire ring. All of the sites are located on the shoreline of the river. A water pump, a fish-cleaning shack, and vault toilets are also provided. No fee is charged for overnight camping.

Picnic Area: A few tables and two shelters are provided for picnicking.

Water Recreation: Two concrete boat ramps provide easy river access for all sizes of motorboats. Fishing for walleyes is very popular on the Rainy River, and most visitors to this park plan on fishing.

Trails: None.

Recreational Facilities: Older-style playground equipment is provided.

Seasons: The campground is open from April through November each year.

Directions: From International Falls, take State Highway 11 west for 43 miles to Birchdale, then follow the park signs north 1 mile to the park entrance.

36. Rainy River Wayside

This wayside provides a nice spot to stop and gaze at the Rainy River and the Canadian border. It is located adjacent to State Highway 11 in northern Koochiching County.

Camping: None.

Picnic Area: The picnic area contains a few tables, grills, and a fire ring. A vault toilet is also provided.

Water Recreation: The wayside provides a view of the Rainy River but no developed shoreline or boat access.

Trails: None.

Recreational Facilities: None.

Seasons: The wayside is open year-round.

Directions: From International Falls, take State Highway 11 west for 64 miles; the wayside is on the right side of the highway.

37. Samuelson Park

Quietly nestled in the southeastern corner of Koochiching County, this small park offers carry-in access to the Littlefork River.

Camping: None.

Picnic Area: None.

Water Recreation: Carry-in canoe or small-boat access to the Littlefork River is provided.

Trails: None.

Recreational Facilities: None.

Seasons: The park is open year-round.

Directions: From International Falls, take U.S. Highway 71 south for 17 miles to State Highway 65 in Littlefork; then take State Highway 65 south for 42 miles and County Road 75 east for 3 miles.

Lake County

There are no county parks in Lake County.

Lake of the Woods County

Highway Department
PO Box 808
Baudette, MN 56623
(218) 634-1767

38. Graceton Beach County Park

Lake of the Woods is a vast expanse of water that extends as far as the eye can see from this small park, which is located in the far northern part of the state. It offers a scenic site for a picnic or swim on a warm summer day.

Camping: None.

Picnic Area: Facilities include a shelter, picnic tables, a water pump, and a vault toilet.

Water Recreation: A nice swimming beach provides access to the waters of Lake of the Woods.

Trails: None.

Recreational Facilities: None.

Seasons: The park is open from May through September.

Directions: From Baudette, take State Highway 172 north for 10 miles, then County Road 8 west for 3 miles; take County Road 20 north for 1 mile, then continue west on County Road 4 for 2 miles.

Mahnomen County

There are no county parks in Mahnomen County.

Marshall County

Florian Park
28219 380th Street NW
Stephen, MN 56757
(218) 478-3658

39. Florian Park

Florian Park offers camping and water recreation activities in northwestern Minnesota. It holds the distinction of being the farthest county park in the northwestern part of the state, and unofficially it is the farthest park from the state capital, Saint Paul.

Camping: The campground features 78 sites that include electric and water hookups, tables, and fire rings. A large, grassy open area provides ample room for tents. Other facilities include restrooms with showers, an RV dump station, and a camp store. A fee is charged for overnight camping.

Picnic Area: The picnic area includes four shelters, picnic tables, and grills.

Water Recreation: The main attraction of this park is the Tamarac River impoundment, which provides canoeing, fishing, and swimming opportunities.

Amenities include carry-in canoe access, a sandy swimming beach, and a handicap-accessible fishing pier. Paddleboat rentals are also available.

Trails: None.

Recreational Facilities: Other amenities include a unique three-hole golf course, playground equipment, a volleyball court, horseshoe pits, a basketball court, and a ball field.

Seasons: The park is open from early May through early September.

Directions: From Warren, take U.S. Highway 75 north for 17 miles to County Road 6, turn right (east) and drive for 10 miles; turn right and take County Road 138 south for 1 mile to the park entrance. A vehicle permit is required for entry into the park.

Mille Lacs County

There are no county parks in Mille Lacs County.

Morrison County

Public Works
1208 West River Road
Little Falls, MN 56345
(320) 632-0121

40. Belle Prairie County Park

River, forest, and prairie combine at a historic site along the Mississippi River, which is preserved within the borders of this park. It provides a nice day-use destination or a wayside rest for picnicking and river access.

Camping: None.

Picnic Area: Under the watchful eyes of towering white pines, the picnic area features a shelter, numerous tables, grills, and vault toilets.

Water Recreation: A concrete boat ramp provides boat and canoe access to the Mississippi River. Fishing from shore or boat is possible in several locations. The park also provides a couple of canoe wayside rests.

Trails: Grassy hiking trails loop through the park, and a short trail follows the main riverbank.

Recreational Facilities: Playground equipment, horseshoe pits, and an open field are provided.

Seasons: The park is open year-round.

Directions: From Little Falls, take State Highway 371 north for 3 miles; the park entrance is on the left side of the highway.

(To read more about the park, see "25 Favorite County Parks" in the first section of this guide.)

Norman County

There are no county parks in Norman County.

Otter Tail County

Highway Department
419 Court Street South
Fergus Falls, MN 56537
(218) 998-8470
www.co.ottertail.mn.us/phelpsmill/

41. Phelps Mill County Park

The history of flour milling in rural Minnesota is preserved and the story of one such rural mill is told at Phelps Mill County Park. The Ottertail River, which once provided the means for milling wheat into flour, now provides the backdrop for a scenic picnic area and interpretive history site. Locals celebrate this history every July with the Phelps Mill Festival.

Camping: None.

Picnic Area: A large picnic area with numerous picnic tables, two picnic shelters, vault toilets, and two fire rings provided.

Water Recreation: Visitors can fish from the shoreline of the Otter Tail River.

Trails: None.

Recreational Facilities: Older-style playground equipment is provided in the picnic area. The Phelps Mill is on the National Register of Historic Places and is open daily to allow visitors to explore and learn about the site's flour-milling history. The seven-minute video, *A River of Wheat,* can be viewed in the mill. All four levels of the mill contain authentic machinery, along with interpretive panels explaining the machinery's functions.

Seasons: The park and mill are open from April through October.

Directions: From Fergus Falls, take County Road 27 north for 5 miles, then turn right and go east on County Road 10 for 4 miles; the road then turns into County Road 1. Continue east on County Road 1 for 7.50 miles, then turn left and go north, following the park signs.

(To read more about the park, see "25 Favorite County Parks" in the first section of this guide.)

Pennington County

County Courthouse
101 Main Avenue North
Thief River Falls, MN 56701
(218) 683-7000

42. Oakland Park

Large hardwood trees distinguish the landscape of this park, which is located within the city of Thief River Falls. It is primarily used for picnics and large outdoor gatherings.

Camping: None.

Picnic Area: Two large shelters and numerous picnic tables offer ample

Volleyball and horseshoes are two of the many activities at Oakland Park.

room for large numbers of picnickers. Handicap-accessible vault toilets are also provided.

Water Recreation: None.

Trails: A river walk trail begins at Oakland Park.

Recreational Facilities: Older-style playground equipment, athletic fields, a ball field, horseshoe pits, and sand volleyball courts are provided.

Seasons: The park is open from May through September.

Directions: From State Highway 32 on the south side of Thief River Falls, turn east onto County Road 76 and go one-half mile to Oakland Park Road; the park entrance is to the right.

Pine County

There are no county parks in Pine County.

Polk County

Highway Department
820 Old Highway 75 South
Crookston, MN 56716
(218) 281-3952

43. East Shore Park

With a county road located so close to Maple Lake, it seemed natural to convert the small strip of land into a roadside park. It is a small day-use site with a long stretch of sandy shoreline.

Camping: None.

Picnic Area: Several picnic tables are provided in the grassy picnic area. Two small picnic shelters provide the only shade, because the park's trees are very small. Portable toilets are also provided, including one that is handicap-accessible.

Water Recreation: Maple Lake features swimming and a variety of boating opportunities. A portion of the park's long sandy beach is designated for swimming and marked with buoys. Boat access to the lake is provided by two concrete boat ramps. A handicap-accessible floating fishing pier is also provided.

Trails: None.

Recreational Facilities: None.

Seasons: The park is open year-round.

Directions: From Crookston, take U.S. Highway 2 east for 20 miles, turn right and go south on County Road 10 for 3 miles; the park is on the right ride of the road.

44. Maple Lake County Park

The park includes a campground and picnic area that overlook Maple Lake.

Camping: The campground features 20 campsites with electricity that can accommodate both tent and RV-style camping. Each includes a fire ring and a picnic table. Restrooms with showers, two portable toilets, one handicap-accessible portable toilet, and an RV dump station are also provided. The park office is staffed during the season, and a fee is charged for overnight camping.

Picnic Area: A large shelter and several picnic tables are provided.

Water Recreation: Maple Lake offers fishing and boating opportunities. A dirt/sand boat ramp and small sand beach are provided.

Trails: None.

Recreational Facilities: None.

Seasons: The park is open from May through September.

Directions: From Crookston, take U.S. Highway 2 east for 20 miles, then turn right and go south on County Road 12 for 3.50 miles; the park is on the left side of the road.

45. Tilberg County Park

Tilberg County Park sits among a thick stand of hardwood trees overlooking Cross Lake in the rolling farmland of northwest Minnesota. It offers locals and visitors a quiet retreat for camping and fishing.

Camping: The campground features 16 shaded campsites that can accommodate both tent and RV camping. Each includes a fire ring and a picnic table. A few sites also offer electricity and water. A campground host oversees the campground during the summer season. Two portable toilets, one handicap-accessible portable toilet, and an RV dump station are also provided. A fee is charged for overnight camping.

Picnic Area: A medium-sized picnic shelter is located on the edge of the campground and overlooks Cross Lake. Several picnic tables are provided.

Water Recreation: Cross Lake offers fishing and boating opportunities. A dirt/sand boat ramp is provided for small-boat launching, and a handicap-accessible, floating fishing pier offers a shoreline fishing option.

Trails: None.

Recreational Facilities: None.

Seasons: The park is open from May through September.

Directions: From Crookston, take U.S. Highway 2 east for 44 miles to Fosston, then turn left on County Road 6 and go north for 3 miles. Turn right on County Road 3 and go 5 miles east and north to County Road 29; turn right and follow the signs.

Pope County

There are no county parks in Pope County.

Red Lake County

County Courthouse
124 Langevin Avenue
Red Lake Falls, MN 56750
(218) 253-2697

46. Old Crossing Treaty Park

This park has a lot of historical significance. It marks the site of the Red Lake River crossing on the old Saint Paul Ox-Cart Trail extending from Saint Paul to

Plenty of history and access to the Red Lake River are found at Old Crossing Treaty Park.

Pembina. It was also the site where a treaty was signed in 1863 that ceded the Red River Valley territory to the United States.

Camping: Ten primitive campsites feature tables and fire rings. A water pump and vault toilets are also provided. No fee is charged for camping.

Picnic Area: Visitors can picnic in the park at any of the available picnic tables.

Water Recreation: A large concrete ramp provides small-boat access to the Red Lake River.

Trails: None.

Recreational Facilities: None.

Seasons: The park is open year-round.

Directions: From the town of Red Lake Falls, take County Road 11 west for 7.50 miles, then turn right on County Road 3 and go 1 mile; just after crossing the bridge, turn right onto a gravel road and follow the county park signs.

Roseau County

There are no county parks in Roseau County.

Saint Louis County

There are no county parks in Saint Louis County.

Stearns County

Parks Department
1802 County Road 137
Waite Park, MN 56387
(320) 255-6172
www.co.stearns.mn.us/departments/parks

47. Lake Sylvia County Park

Shoreline fishing is the highlight of this small lakeside park. Located in north-central Stearns County, it features lakeside picnicking and shoreline fishing—all on only three acres.

Camping: None.

Picnic Area: Tables and grills are provided.

Water Recreation: A floating fishing pier is provided. A small-boat ramp is located near the park to provide access to Lake Sylvia.

Trails: None.

Recreational Facilities: None.

Seasons: The park is open year-round.

Directions: From Saint Cloud, take Interstate 94 about 35 miles west to Melrose, turn right and go north on County Road 13 for 4 miles, then turn right and go east on County Road 17 for 1 mile.

48. Mississippi River County Park

This large park features about a mile of Mississippi River shoreline and several acres of forest and prairie. It sits on the opposite shore of the river from Benton County's Graves Farm Park. Together these two parks preserve a large tract of river frontage in a rapidly developing area along the Mississippi River.

Camping: None.

Picnic Area: The first picnic area is located adjacent to the boat access on the shore of the river. Peaceful views of the river and six picnic tables and grills are provided. The second picnic area is located inland from the river and features a picnic shelter, a water pump, several tables and grills, and vault toilets, all within the friendly shade of oak and cedar trees.

Water Recreation: A public boat access to the river features a concrete ramp and medium-sized parking lot. A portable toilet is also provided for both ramp users and picnickers.

Trails: Several miles of grassy hiking/skiing trails wind through the interior and along the river shoreline of the park.

Recreational Facilities: The inland picnic area features older-style playground equipment, volleyball areas, horseshoe pits, and a large grassy activity field.

Seasons: The park is open year-round.

Directions: From Saint Cloud, take County Road 1 north for 5 miles to Sartell, then continue on County Road 1 for another 6 miles; the park entrance is on the right side of the road.

49. Quarry Park and Nature Preserve

Emerald-green ponds of water encased in red granite await visitors to Quarry Park. Formally an industrial quarry, it now features a regenerated forest, prairies, and unique, water-filled quarries. A variety of recreational opportunities are provided.

Camping: None.

Picnic Area: Located at the trailhead, the picnic area features a medium-sized

Sterns Swim Deck in Quarry Park and Nature Preserve.

shelter, picnic tables, a handicap-accessible portable toilet, and a restored native prairie area.

Water Recreation: Ten former granite quarries are now filled with water and provide various opportunities. Swimming is allowed in only one quarry. A swim dock is provided, but the swimming is unguarded. Fishing is allowed only in designated quarries. Scuba diving is also allowed in a couple of quarries.

Trails: Two miles of hiking/skiing trails will take you to scenic overlooks and quarries. An equal length of a mountain-biking trails are also provided.

Recreational Facilities: None.

Seasons: The park is open year-round.

Directions: From Saint Cloud, take State Highway 23 west a short distance to 10th Avenue, turn left and go south to the first stop sign; turn right and go west on County Road 137 for almost 1 mile to the park entrance on the left side of the road. A vehicle permit fee is charged for entry into the park.

(To read more about the park, see "25 Favorite County Parks" in the first section of this guide.)

50. Spring Hill County Park

Over 80 acres of natural shoreline, prairie, and forest make up the landscape of Spring Hill County Park. Groups of visitors also can enjoy the picnic facilities and carry-in access to the Sauk River.

Camping: None

Picnic Area: Facilities include a large shelter, picnic tables, a grill, and vault toilets near the parking lot; there are also two picnic tables and grills near the river.

Water Recreation: Carry-in canoe access to the Sauk River is possible from the parking lot.

Trails: A few grassy trails lead down to the river.

Recreational Facilities: Older-style playground equipment is provided.

Seasons: The park is open year-round.

Directions: From Saint Cloud, take State Highway 23 about 21 miles southwest to Richmond; then after heading 2 miles west of Richmond, turn right and head northwest on County Road 12 for 8 miles.

51. Upper Spunk Lake County Park

This park provides carry-in access and picnicking opportunities on Upper "Big" Spunk Lake. It is a small site located on a backwater channel of the lake amid lowland Elm and Birch trees.

Camping: None.

Picnic Area: A couple of picnic tables and a campfire ring are provided for visitor use.

Water Recreation: Access for shoreline fishing is limited on the main lake due to tall, marshy grasses. It is possible to carry a canoe and launch on the backwater channel to gain access to the main lake.

Trails: None.

Recreational Facilities: None.

Seasons: The park is open year-round.

Directions: From Saint Cloud, take Interstate 94 west for 19 miles to the Avon exit; from there, take County Road 9 south for nearly 2 miles; the park entrance is on the left side of the road.

52. Warner Lake County Park

Surrounding Warner Lake, this park features a large picnic area and trails. A nature center is home to interpretive programs and can also be reserved for large groups. The picnic area and beach attract numerous visitors on summer days.

Camping: None.

Picnic Area: Facilities include a large shelter, two medium shelters, picnic tables, grills, electricity, and handicap-accessible vault toilets.

Water Recreation: A large swimming beach, floating fishing pier, and concrete boat ramp provide boating, fishing, and swimming access to Warner Lake.

Trails: Four miles of paved and gravel hiking/skiing trails can be found within the park.

Recreational Facilities: None.

Seasons: The park is open from May through September.

Directions: From Saint Cloud, take County Road 7 south for 4 miles to where the road turns into County Road 44; stay on County Road 44 for 4 miles, following the park signs.

Stevens County

There are no county parks in Stevens County.

Todd County

County Courthouse
221 First Avenue South
Long Prairie, MN 56347
(320) 732-6447
www.co.todd.mn.us

53. Battle Point Park

Although it doesn't feature many amenities, this park provides boat access and preserves open space on the northern end of Lake Osakis. It is most popular for motorboat access to the lake.

Camping: None.

Picnic Area: A few picnic tables are provided.

Water Recreation: A concrete boat ramp provides boating and fishing access to Lake Osakis.

Trails: None.

Recreational Facilities: None.

Seasons: The park is open year-round.

Directions: From Long Prairie, take U.S. Highway 71 south for 2 miles, turn right and go west on County Road 10 for 8 miles; turn left and go south on County Road 37 for 1 mile, then turn right and go west on 210th Street for 2 miles to the end of the road, where you will see the park entrance.

Traverse County

Highway Department
702 2nd Avenue North
Wheaton, MN 56296
(320) 563-4652

54. Pete's Park

This park is named after a local game warden. It is a small wayside area that provides dispersed camping and carry-in small-boat access to the Mustinka River.

Camping: None.

Picnic Area: On the east side of the river, a picnic table and some benches are provided. The west side of the river features vault toilets, a parking lot, and carry-in access to the river.

Water Recreation: There is a carry-in access for canoes or small boats along the Mustinka River for visitors' fishing or hunting activities.

Trails: None.

Recreational Facilities: None.

Seasons: The park is open year-round.

Directions: From Wheaton, take County Road 27 southwest for 6 miles to State Highway 117 and turn right; the park is located on both sides of the river next to the Highway 117 bridge.

55. Traverse County Park

From this park, visitors have access to the unique and scenic Lake Traverse in west-central Minnesota. The Lake Traverse Reservoir, straddling the Minnesota–South Dakota border, was created and is maintained by the U.S. Army Corps of Engineers for flood control and recreation purposes.

Camping: The campground features nine sites (five with electricity), and each includes a picnic table and a fire ring. Four vault toilets are also provided. A fee is charged for overnight camping.

Picnic Area: In addition to the campsites, the park also offers several picnic tables and three small shelters.

Water Recreation: A concrete boat ramp provides access to Lake Traverse for all sizes of motorized and nonmotorized boats. The shoreline of the park is primarily rock, but a small bay is designed to allow overnight beaching of small boats for campers. Also, a small unsupervised swimming beach is provided.

Trails: None.

Recreational Facilities: None.

Seasons: The campground is open from May through October.

Directions: From Wheaton, take County Road 27 southwest for 18 miles to the park entrance on the right side of the road.

Wadena County

Parks Department
415 South Jefferson Street
Wadena, MN 56482
(651) 631-7604
www.co.wadena.mn.us

Wadena County features ten parks located along the Crow Wing River, which are designed for use along the river canoe route. Most of them feature a forested shoreline and dispersed camping facilities. A fee is charged for overnight camping. These parks are intended for the convenience of people on the river, and thus they are very small, with few amenities; also, they are not easily accessible by road. As a result, driving directions have been provided for only one of them (Old Wadena County Park).

56. Anderson's Crossing

Camping: A fire ring, water, and an outdoor latrine are provided.

Picnic Area: A picnic table is provided.

Water Recreation: Canoeing and fishing is available on the Crow Wing River.

Trails: None.

Recreational Facilities: None.

Seasons: The park is open year-round.

Directions: This park is located 14 miles downstream from Tree Farm Landing and 7 miles upstream from Frame's Landing.

57. Bullard Bluff

Camping: A fire ring, water, and an outdoor latrine are provided.

Picnic Area: A picnic table is provided.

Water Recreation: Canoeing and fishing are available on the Crow Wing River.
Trails: None.
Recreational Facilities: None.
Seasons: The park is open year-round.
Directions: This park is located 6 miles downstream from Cottingham and 4 miles upstream from Old Wadena.

58. Cottingham County Park

Camping: A fire ring, water, and an outdoor latrine are provided.
Picnic Area: A picnic table is provided.
Water Recreation: Canoeing and fishing are available on the Crow Wing River.
Trails: None.
Recreational Facilities: None.
Seasons: The park is open year-round.
Directions: This park is located 4 miles downstream from Knob Hill and 6 miles upstream from Bullard Bluff.

59. Frame's Landing

Camping: A fire ring, water, and an outdoor latrine are provided.
Picnic Area: A picnic table is provided.
Water Recreation: Canoeing and fishing are available on the Crow Wing River.
Trails: None.
Recreational Facilities: None.
Seasons: The park is open year-round.
Directions: This park is located 1 mile downstream from Stigman's Mound and 6 miles upstream from Little White Dog.

60. Knob Hill

Camping: A fire ring, water, and an outdoor latrine are provided.
Picnic Area: A picnic table is provided.
Water Recreation: Canoeing and fishing are available on the Crow Wing River.
Trails: None.
Recreational Facilities: None.
Seasons: The park is open year-round.
Directions: This park is located 6 miles downstream from Little White Dog and 3 miles upstream from Cottingham.

61. Little White Dog

Camping: A fire ring, water, and an outdoor latrine are provided.
Picnic Area: A picnic table is provided.
Water Recreation: Canoeing and fishing are available on the Crow Wing River.
Trails: None.
Recreational Facilities: None.
Seasons: The park is open year-round.
Directions: The park is located 6 miles downstream from Frame's Landing and 6 miles upstream from Knob Hill.

62. McGivern County Park

Camping: A fire ring, water, and an outdoor latrine are provided.
Picnic Area: A picnic table is provided.
Water Recreation: Canoeing and fishing are available on the Crow Wing River.
Trails: None.
Recreational Facilities: None.
Seasons: The park is open year-round.
Directions: The park is located 2 miles downstream from Old Wadena; this is the last Wadena County park on the river.

63. Old Wadena County Park

With more than 200 acres of land on the Crow Wing River, Old Wadena is the largest park in the Wadena County system. It marks the first site of the town of Wadena and has historical significance for Native Americans.

Camping: Fire rings, water, and an outdoor latrine are provided.
Picnic Area: This park is commonly used for picnics, and tables are provided.
Water Recreation: Canoeing and fishing are available on the Crow Wing River.
Trails: None.
Recreational Facilities: None.
Seasons: The park is open year-round.
Directions: This park is located 4 miles downstream from Bullard's Bluff and 2 miles upstream from McGivern. From Wadena, take County Road 4 east for 11 miles, continue east on County Road 123 for 3 miles, and take County Road 29 south for 1 mile.

64. Stigman's Mound County Park

Camping: None.

Picnic Area: A small shelter and picnic tables are provided.
Water Recreation: Canoeing and fishing are available on the Crow Wing River.
Trails: None.
Recreational Facilities: None.
Seasons: The park is open year-round.
Directions: This park is located 6 miles downstream from Anderson's Crossing and 1 mile upstream from Frame's Landing.

65. Tree Farm Landing

Camping: A fire ring, water, and an outdoor latrine are provided.
Picnic Area: A picnic table is provided.
Water Recreation: Canoeing and fishing are available on the Crow Wing River.
Trails: None.
Recreational Facilities: None.
Seasons: The park is open year-round.
Directions: This is the first Wadena County Park on the canoe route. It is located 14 miles upstream from Anderson's Crossing.

Wilkin County

There are no county parks in Wilkin County.

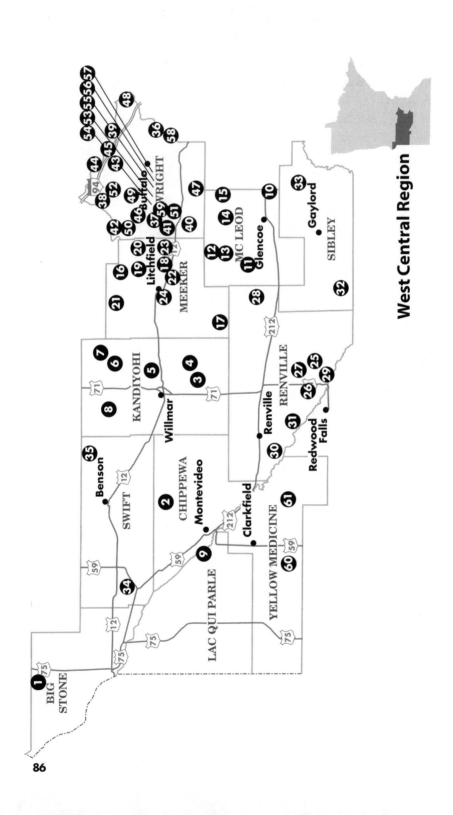

West Central Region

WEST-CENTRAL REGION

Big Stone County

County Courthouse
20 SE 2nd Street
Ortonville, MN 56278
(320) 839-2594

1. Toqua Park

This park is located on the southern shore of East Toqua Lake near Graceville in northern Big Stone County. The entire park is developed and includes a campground, a picnic area, and baseball fields.

Camping: Twelve RV sites and two tent sites are all located on the shore of the lake. Each site is named after a lake or town in the county and includes a fire ring and a picnic table. A restroom building with showers is located a short walk from the campsites. A fee is charged for camping.

Picnic Area: The picnic area features several picnic tables and grills and includes two shelters.

Camp or picnic by the lake at Toqua Park.

Water Recreation: A concrete boat ramp provides access to East Toqua Lake for all sizes of motorized and nonmotorized boats. An undesignated swimming beach is also located near the boat access.

Trails: None.

Recreational Facilities: A large playground is located next to the picnic area and features older-style playground equipment. The park also features two baseball fields and related amenities, which are utilized by the nearby town of Graceville.

Seasons: The campground is open from May through September.

Directions: From Ortonville, take U.S. Highway 75 north for 17.5 miles to County Road 18, then turn left and head west for a half mile. The park entrance is on the left-hand side of the road between the park and the golf course.

Chippewa County

Auditor's Office
629 North 11th Street
Montevideo, MN 56265
(320) 269-7447
www.co.chippewa.mn.us

2. Buffalo Lake County Park

Located in north-central Chippewa County, this park offers day-use opportunities under the thick cover of hardwood trees. Buffalo Lake provides a scenic backdrop for picnics and water recreation.

Camping: None.

Picnic Area: Facilities include a shelter, picnic tables, and portable toilets.

Water Recreation: Buffalo Lake provides a scenic backdrop to the park's landscape with boating and fishing opportunities. A small-boat ramp provides access to the lake.

Trails: None.

Recreational Facilities: Older-style playground equipment is provided.

Seasons: The park is open from May through September.

Directions: From Montevideo, take State Highway 7 east for 11 miles, then turn left and go north on State Highway 277 for 11 miles to where it turns into County Road 4; continue north on County Road 4 for 2 miles.

Kandiyohi County

County Parks
400 SW Benson Avenue
Willmar, MN 56201
(320) 231-6202
www.co.kandiyohi.mn.us

3. County Park 1

Overlooking the west side of Big Kandiyohi Lake, this park features one of the largest campgrounds in the county. It is also a popular location for swimming and boat access on the lake.

Camping: Facilities include 90 RV/tent sites with electricity and restrooms with showers. At least 50 percent of the campsites are utilized for long-term camping. A fee is charged for overnight camping and a caretaker lives on-site; call (320) 995-6599 for reservations and information.

Picnic Area: Picnic tables, grills, and a portable toilet are provided in two picnic areas.

Water Recreation: Big Kandiyohi Lake features excellent fishing and boating opportunities. A swimming beach and boat ramp provide access to the lake. Boats and motors can be rented.

Trails: None.

Recreational Facilities: A modern play structure is provided.

Seasons: The park is open from May through September.

Directions: From Willmar, take U.S. Highway 71 south for 7 miles, turn left and go east on County Road 3 for 3 miles, then turn right and go south on County Road 44 for 2 miles.

4. County Park 2

A nicely shaded campground with large sites is provided for campers at this park. It is located on the east side of Big Kandiyohi Lake and also features a large sandy swimming beach.

Camping: Facilities include 90 RV/tent sites with electricity, some portable toilets, restrooms with showers, and an RV dump station. A fee is charged for overnight camping and a caretaker lives on-site; call (320) 664-4707 for reservations and information.

Picnic Area: A shelter, picnic tables, and grills are provided.

There's plenty of shade for campers at County Park 2 in Kandiyohi County.

Water Recreation: Big Kandiyohi Lake features excellent fishing, swimming, and boating opportunities. Access to the lake is provided by a concrete boat ramp or sandy swimming beach. Boats and motors can be rented.

Trails: None.

Recreational Facilities: A modern play structure is provided.

Seasons: The park is open from May through September.

Directions: From Willmar, take U.S. Highway 71 south for 7 miles, turn left and go east on County Road 3 for 4.5 miles, then turn right and go east on 90th Ave. SE for four miles; turn right and go south on County Road 8 for 2 miles, following the signs to the park.

5. County Park 3

Similar to its sister parks, this park features a modern campground with hookups. It is located on Diamond Lake, and access to the lake is provided. A fully stocked store can supply anything a camper may have forgotten to bring.

Camping: Facilities include 80 RV/tent sites with electricity, restrooms with showers, and an RV dump station. A fee is charged for overnight camping and a caretaker lives on-site; call (320) 974-8520 for reservations and information.

Picnic Area: Picnic tables and grills are provided in both picnic areas. One picnic area also includes two shelters and toilets.

Water Recreation: Diamond Lake offers swimming, fishing, and boating opportunities. Park facilities include a concrete boat ramp and a sandy beach. Boats and motors can be rented.

Trails: None.

Recreational Facilities: Playground equipment is provided.

Seasons: The park is open from May through September.

Directions: From Willmar, take U.S. Highway 12 east for 9 miles, then turn left and go north on County Road 4 for 4 miles.

6. County Park 4

From the park, the county provides general public access to Green Lake, which is popular for boating, fishing, and swimming. It is a day-use area located within the town of Spicer.

Camping: None.

Picnic Area: A medium-sized shelter, picnic tables, grills, and portable toilets (one is handicap-accessible) are provided.

Water Recreation: A large swimming beach is supervised by lifeguards during the summer. Adjacent concrete boat ramps provide boating and fishing access to Green Lake.

Trails: None.

Recreational Facilities: None.

Seasons: The park is open during the summer months.

Directions: From Willmar, take U.S. Highway 71 north for 5 miles to State Highway 23, turn right and continue east and north for 4.50 miles to Indian Beach Road in Spicer; then turn right again. The park will be immediately on the left side of the road.

7. County Park 5

With a small amount of land and numerous modern campsites, this park is designed for those who want to spend a weekend or week on the lake. Boating and swimming access to Green Lake is also provided.

Camping: Facilities include 54 RV/tent sites with electricity, water, and sewer hookups, an RV dump station, and restrooms with showers. A fee is charged for overnight camping and a caretaker lives on-site; call (320) 796-5564 for reservations and information.

Picnic Area: Two shelters, picnic tables, and handicap-accessible restrooms near the beach are provided.

Water Recreation: Green Lake offers excellent swimming, fishing, and boating opportunities. Park facilities include a concrete boat ramp and a sandy beach. Boats and motors can be rented.

Trails: A paved bicycle trail connects this park to the nearby communities of New London and Spicer as well as the Glacial Lake Trail.

Recreational Facilities: A modern play structure is provided.

Seasons: The park is open from April 1 to October 1 each year.

Directions: From Willmar, take U.S. Highway 71 north for 5 miles to State Highway 23, turn right and continue east and north for 6 miles to North Shore Drive; then turn right and go east for 4 miles.

8. County Park 7

Family camping and fun is the name of the game at this park, which features several amenities on Games Lake. It is located adjacent to Sibley State Park in northern Kandiyohi County.

Camping: Facilities include 52 RV/tent sites with electricity, an RV dump station, and handicap-accessible restrooms with showers. A fee is charged for overnight camping and a caretaker lives on-site; call (320) 354-4453 for reservations and information.

Picnic Area: Two shelters, picnic tables, grills, and portable toilets are provided near the beach.

Water Recreation: Games Lake offers excellent swimming, fishing, and boating opportunities. Park facilities include a concrete boat ramp and sandy beach that is supervised by lifeguards during the summer. Boats and motors can be rented.

Trails: None.

Recreational Facilities: A modern play structure and a volleyball court are provided.

Seasons: The park is open from May through September.

Directions: From Willmar, take U.S. Highway 71 north for 14 miles, then turn left and go west on State Highway 9 for 3.50 miles to County Road 5; turn left and go south for 1 mile.

Lac Qui Parle County

County Courthouse
600 6th Street
Madison, MN 56256
(320) 598-7444

9. Lac Qui Parle County Park

Lac Qui Parle County Park encompasses several acres of undeveloped land along the Lac Qui Parle River. It has been left primarily in its natural state, preserving the mixed hardwood forest of the Lac Qui Parle River valley. Visitors will find a park road and a few user-developed trails.

Camping: None.

Picnic Area: Several large grassy areas are maintained and mowed so it is possible to have an informal picnic at this park. However, there are no tables or restroom facilities.

Water Recreation: From this park, visitors can access the Lac Qui Parle River from the shoreline, and they may also carry in small watercraft.

Lac Qui Parle County Park has been left largely in its natural state.

Trails: A few trails wind their way through the park's landscape.

Recreational Facilities: None.

Seasons: The park is open year-round.

Directions: From Madison, take County Road 20 east for 13 miles, then take County Road 31 south for 4.0 miles. From here, follow the county park signs by taking a right-hand turn onto a gravel road; the signs will take you 2 miles west, then 1 mile north, and a half mile west again to the park entrance.

McLeod County

Park Department
840 Century Avenue, Suite B
Hutchinson, MN 55350
(320) 587-0770
www.co.mcleod.mn.us

10. Buffalo Creek County Park

The forested banks of the Buffalo Creek create a scenic backdrop for this small park. It makes a nice rest stop when traveling on busy U.S. Highway 212.

Camping: None.

Picnic Area: A shelter, picnic tables, grills, and vault toilets are provided.

Water Recreation: None.

Trails: A short trail follows the creek.

Recreational Facilities: A few swings and an open ball field are available for use.

Seasons: The park is open from May 1 through October 1.

Directions: From Hutchinson, take State Highway 22 for 14 miles southeast to Glencoe, turn left on Highway 212 and go east for 2 miles; the park entrance is on the right side of the road.

11. Lake Marion Park

Opened in 1981, this park is 86 acres in size and unofficially it ranks as the most popular campground in McLeod County. Its close proximity to Hutchinson provides easy access to a variety of recreational opportunities for campers.

Camping: Numerous RV and tent campsites, a restroom/shower building, and an RV dump station are provided. A fee is charged for overnight camping, and park caretakers live on-site.

Picnic Area: Two shelters, picnic tables, and grills are provided.

Water Recreation: A concrete ramp with a dock and a floating fishing pier provide access to Lake Marion for fishing and boating opportunities, while swimmers can enjoy the unsupervised sandy beach.

Trails: A 1-mile-long trail offers the opportunity for hiking and skiing.

Recreational Facilities: Other facilities include playground equipment, a volleyball court, and a softball field.

Seasons: The park is open from May 1 through October 1.

Directions: From Hutchinson, take State Highway 15 south for 6 miles; the park entrance is on the right side of the road.

12. Piepenburg Park

As one of McLeod County's favorite camping destinations, this park features open meadows and forested lakeshore on Belle Lake in the northwestern corner of the county. A nice sandy beach and a boat ramp also draw many visitors to the park for day-use activities.

Camping: Approximately 21 RV/tent sites with electrical hookups are provided. The campground also includes a restroom/shower building. A fee is charged for overnight camping, and park caretakers live on-site.

Picnic Area: Shelters, picnic tables, grills, and pit toilets are provided in two picnic areas.

Water Recreation: A concrete ramp with a dock provides access to Belle Lake for fishing and boating opportunities, while swimmers can enjoy a sandy beach.

Trails: None.

Recreational Facilities: A modern play structure is provided near the campground and beach.

Seasons: The park is open from May 1 through October 1.

Directions: From Hutchinson, take State Highway 15 north for 7 miles, then turn left and go west on County Road 60 for 3 miles; the park entrance is on the right side of the road.

13. Stahl's Lake County Park

Hiking and skiing trails are provided at this park. Situated between Stahl's and French Lakes, the trails weave through a mixed hardwood forest and generally are very quiet.

Camping: None.

Picnic Area: Facilities include a shelter, picnic tables, grills, and vault toilets.

Water Recreation: A nearby boat ramp provides access to Stahl's Lake.

Trails: Nearly 2 miles of hiking/skiing trails wind through the landscape of this small park.

Recreational Facilities: None.

Seasons: The park is open year-round.

Directions: From Hutchinson, take State Highway 15 north for 6 miles, then turn left and go west on County Road 73 for 3 miles; the park entrance is on the left side of the road.

14. Swan Lake County Park

Large oak and elm trees tower over the landscape of this park. Boat access to Swan Lake and picnic facilities are provided.

Camping: None.

Picnic Area: Facilities include a large shelter, picnic tables, grills, and vault toilets.

Water Recreation: Boating and fishing access is provided, along with a concrete ramp, a dock, and a handicap-accessible floating fishing pier.

Trails: None.

Recreational Facilities: None.

Seasons: The park is open from May 1 through October 1.

Directions: From Hutchinson, take State Highway 7 east for 9 miles, then turn left and go west on County Road 16 for 1 mile; the park is located on the east shore of Swan Lake.

15. William May County Park

If you are looking for a quiet, secluded picnic location in McLeod County, William May County Park might be the place. A small picnic area with limited facilities is provided.

Picnic Area: A shelter, picnic tables, grills, and vault toilets are provided.

Camping: None.

Water Recreation: None.

Trails: None.

Recreational Facilities: None.

Seasons: The park is open from May 1 through October 1.

Directions: From Hutchinson, take State Highway 7 east for approximately 18 miles, turn left and go north on Zebra Avenue for 4 miles, then turn left and go west on 30th Street for 1 mile; the park is on the right side of the road.

Meeker County

Parks Department
325 North Sibley Ave.
Litchfield, MN 55355
(320) 693-5450
www.co.meeker.mn.us/departments/park.html

16. Clear Lake County Park

This is a small wooded park on the edge of Clear Lake in northeastern Meeker County. It provides lake access and picnicking opportunities.

Camping: None.

Picnic Area: A small shelter, picnic tables, grills, and vault toilet facilities are provided.

Water Recreation: Motorized and nonmotorized boating and fishing access to Clear Lake is provided, including a concrete boat ramp and a handicap-accessible fishing pier.

Trails: A short trail provides hiking opportunities within the forested landscape of the park.

Recreational Facilities: None.

Seasons: The park is open year-round.

Directions: From Litchfield, go north on State Highway 24 for 11 miles, then turn left and continue north on County Road 2 for 7 miles; watch for the park entrance.

17. Cosmos County Park

Located on Thompson Lake, this small park provides a quiet, off-the-beaten-path location for a picnic or fishing. A large grassy playing field provides plenty of space for games and activities.

Camping: None.

Picnic Area: Facilities include two shelters, picnic tables, and one handicap-accessible vault toilet.

Water Recreation: Fishing can be enjoyed on Thompson Lake from the fishing dock or shoreline.

Trails: None.

Recreational Facilities: A volleyball court, ball field, and playground equipment are provided.

Seasons: The park is open from May through September.
Directions: From Litchfield, go east on U.S. Highway 12 for 3 miles to County Road 9, then turn right and go south for 5 miles.

18. Dassel/Darwin County Park

This unique wayside rest park features several miles of trails, native prairie, and a high scenic overlook. From the top of the overlook, you can see for a long distance over the rolling terrain of west-central Minnesota.

Camping: None.
Picnic Area: A few picnic tables are located near the parking lot and at the top of the hill/overlook. Handicap-accessible vault toilets are also provided.
Water Recreation: None.
Trails: Seven miles of trails are available for horseback riding, hiking, and skiing.
Recreational Facilities: None.
Seasons: The park is open year-round.
Directions: From Litchfield, go east on U.S. Highway 12 for 6 miles; the park entrance is on the left side of the road.

19. Forest City County Park

Large oak and elm trees tower over the landscape of this park and provide a beautiful setting for park activities. The quiet atmosphere and large playground area makes this a nice stop for a picnic or wayside rest.

Camping: None.
Picnic Area: Facilities include two small shelters, picnic tables, grills, and vault toilets.
Water Recreation: None.
Trails: None.
Recreational Facilities: Older-style playground equipment is provided.
Seasons: The park is open from May through September.
Directions: From Litchfield, go north on State Highway 24 for 11 miles, watching for the park entrance on the left side of the road.

20. Kingston County Park

This small park provides picnicking, fishing, and canoeing opportunities on the North Fork of the Crow River. A gentle and grassy slope along the river makes it ideal for riverbank fishing.

Camping: None.

Picnic Area: A small shelter, picnic tables, grills, and a handicap-accessible vault toilet are provided.

Water Recreation: Fishing and small-boat access is provided by a small dirt ramp.

Trails: None.

Recreational Facilities: Older-style playground equipment is provided.

Seasons: The park is open year-round.

Directions: From Litchfield, go north/northeast on State Highway 24 for 24 miles, turn left, and continue east on County Road 27 for 4 miles; the park entrance is on the right side of the road.

21. Lake Koronis Regional Park

A thick hardwood forest dominates the landscape of this park, which is located on the Stearns and Meeker County line. It features a large picnic area and beach as well as a nice campground. Lake Koronis is a popular boating and fishing destination. This park is a cooperative venture between Meeker and Stearns counties.

Camping: The campground features 37 sites (25 with electricity) with tables

View from the observation tower at Lake Koronis Regional Park.

and fire rings. Restrooms and showers are also provided. A fee is charged for overnight camping, and a park caretaker lives on-site.

Picnic Area: Several picnic tables and grills are provided. In addition, two shelters are available for use. Near the swimming beach, a large shelter and handicap-accessible restrooms round out the amenities.

Water Recreation: A sandy swimming beach provides warm-weather relief. Nearby, a concrete ramp provides boat and fishing access to Lake Koronis.

Trails: Short wooded and paved trails connect the campground, picnic area, and beach.

Recreational Facilities: Playground equipment is provided.

Seasons: The park is open from May through September.

Directions: From Litchfield, go west on U.S. Highway 12 for 9 miles to State Highway 4, turn right and go north for 12 miles, then turn left and go west on County Road 20 for almost 4 miles; the park is on both sides of the road.

22. Lake Manuella County Park

This is a small day-use and swimming area that is quite popular. During the summer, many people utilize the park's sandy beach.

Lake Manuella County Park is a popular swimming destination.

Camping: None.

Picnic Area: A small shelter, picnic tables, grills, and a handicap-accessible vault toilet are provided.

Water Recreation: Activities include swimming in the lake and fishing from the shore. In addition, a boat ramp is provided next to the park.

Trails: None.

Recreational Facilities: None.

Seasons: The park is open year-round.

Directions: From Litchfield, go east on U.S. Highway 12 for 3 miles, then turn right and go south on County Road 9 for 5 miles.

23. Spring Lake County Park

This small day-use park is nestled between rolling hills and small lakes near the small community of Dassel. It features scenic views of the lake from the upper picnic area.

Camping: None.

Picnic Area: Four small shelters, picnic tables, grills, and handicap-accessible vault toilets are provided. The picnic area is split into upper and lower areas of the park.

Spring Lake County Park

Water Recreation: A concrete ramp provides boating and fishing access to Spring Lake.

Trails: None.

Recreational Facilities: A large baseball/softball field gets a lot of summer league use. Older-style playground equipment is also provided.

Seasons: The park is open from May through September.

Directions: From Litchfield, go east on U.S. Highway 12 for 10 miles, turn left and go north on County Road 4 for 1 mile, then turn right and follow the park signs.

24. West Ripley Park

This is a large day-use park located on the shore of Lake Ripley immediately south of Litchfield. It is a favorite picnic destination for large groups.

Camping: None.

Picnic Area: Facilities include an extra-large shelter, picnic tables, grills, and handicap-accessible vault toilets.

Water Recreation: Fishing and boating can be enjoyed on Lake Ripley. A handicap-accessible fishing pier and concrete ramp provide access for those pursuits.

Trails: None.

Recreational Facilities: Older-style playground equipment, a volleyball court, and a tennis court are provided.

Seasons: The park is open from May through September.

Directions: From the center of Litchfield, take County Road 1 south for about 1.5 miles; the park is on the left side of the road.

Renville County

Parks and Recreation
410 East DePue Avenue
Olivia, MN 56277
(320) 523-3768
www.co.renville.mn.us/ecd/park.html

25. Anderson Lake County Park

This is a small day-use park located on the backwaters of the Minnesota River. The only development is a park road and a parking area adjacent to a small pond.

Camping: None.

Picnic Area: None.

Water Recreation: Shoreline fishing on a little pond is available, with a portable toilet on-site.

Trails: None.

Recreational Facilities: None.

Seasons: The park is open year-round.

Directions: From Olivia, take U.S. Highway 71 south for 16 miles, turn left and go east on State Highway 19 for 6 miles to County Road 11; turn right and take that south for 1 mile, then turn left and go east on County Road 5 for 2 miles.

26. Beaver Falls County Park

This park is located near the confluence of Beaver Creek and the Minnesota River. It features forested hills and rocky ravines. A large part of the park has been kept in its natural condition.

Camping: Primitive dispersed camping is allowed in four developed areas of the park. No modern facilities are provided. A fee is charged for overnight camping.

Picnic Area: None.

Water Recreation: None.

Trails: A few miles of hiking trails can be found within the park.

Recreational Facilities: None.

Seasons: The park is open year-round.

Directions: From Olivia, take U.S. Highway 71 south for 14 miles, then turn right and go west on County Road 2 for 3 miles.

27. Birch Coulee County Park

This park is located adjacent to the Birch Coulee Historical Site. In 1862 this area was the site of a battle between the U.S. Army and Dakota Native Americans. The site is within walking distance of the park.

Camping: Primitive dispersed camping is allowed in developed areas of the park. Tables, fire rings, a water pump, and vault toilets are provided. A fee is charged for overnight camping.

Picnic Area: A large shelter, picnic tables, and a handicap-accessible vault toilet is provided.

Water Recreation: None.

Trails: None.

Recreational Facilities: None.

Seasons: The park is open year-round.

Directions: From Olivia, take Highway 71 south for 14 miles, then turn left and go east on County Road 2 for 1 mile to County Road 18; turn right and watch for the park entrance, which is on the same road used to access the Birch Coulee Historical Site.

28. Lake Allie County Park

This is a small campground park located adjacent to Lake Allie in northeastern Renville County. Nearly the entire park is devoted to the campground and picnic area.

Camping: Facilities include 15 RV sites, 5 tent sites, handicap-accessible vault toilets, and an RV dump station. A fee is charged for overnight camping.

Picnic Area: A shelter and picnic tables are provided.

Water Recreation: A concrete boat ramp provides boating and fishing access to Lake Allie.

Trails: None.

Recreational Facilities: None.

Seasons: The park is open from May through September.

Directions: From Olivia, take U.S. Highway 212 east for 18 miles to the town of Buffalo Lake, turn left and go north on County Road 8 for 5 miles to County Road 23; turn right and go east for 1 mile, then take County Road 24 north and east for 2 miles.

29. Mack County Park

This is a relatively undeveloped park on the Minnesota River, which features a historic log cabin site located in the picnic area.

Camping: Dispersed camping is allowed on a few riverside campsites within the park. No facilities except one portable toilet are provided.

Picnic Area: A shelter with only one or two picnic tables and vault toilets are provided.

Water Recreation: Fishing and canoeing access to the Minnesota River are the primary water activities.

Trails: None.

Recreational Facilities: None.

Seasons: The park is open year-round.

Directions: From Olivia, go south on U.S. Highway 71 for 16 miles, then turn left and go east on State Highway 19 for 6 miles; turn right and take County Road 11 south for 1 mile, then turn left and go east on County Road 5 for 7 miles.

30. Skalbekken County Park

Skalbekken is a large, natural-area park with several trails and river access opportunities. It is located in the scenic and historic Minnesota River valley.

Camping: A small campground features eight RV/tent sites and handicap-accessible vault toilets. A fee is charged for overnight camping.

Picnic Area: One shelter with picnic tables and grills is located adjacent to the campground.

Water Recreation: Fishing and carry-in canoe access to the Minnesota River is possible.

Trails: Several miles of hiking and horseback-riding trails are provided within the park.

Recreational Facilities: None.

Seasons: The park is open year-round.

The Minnesota River runs through Skalbekken County Park.

Directions: From Olivia, take U.S. Highway 212 west for 20 miles, then turn left and go south on County Road 10 for 3.5 miles.

31. Vicksburg County Park

Vicksburg is a natural area park located in the Minnesota River valley. It offers dispersed recreation opportunities like camping, fishing, and river access.

Camping: Primitive dispersed camping is allowed in developed areas of the park. Tables, fire rings, and vault toilets are provided. A fee is charged for overnight camping.

Picnic Area: A shelter, picnic tables, and a handicap-accessible vault toilet is provided.

Water Recreation: Carry-in canoeing and fishing access to the Minnesota River is possible in several areas of the park.

Trails: None.

Recreational Facilities: None.

Seasons: The park is open year-round.

Directions: From Olivia, take U.S. Highway 71 south for 7 miles, turn right and go west on County Road 4 for 11 miles, then take County Road 6 south for 2 miles.

Sibley County

Department of Public Works
111 8th Street
Gaylord, MN 55334
(507) 237-4092
www.co.sibley.mn.us

32. Clear Lake County Park

Oak and elm trees characterize the landscape of this park, which also features just over 40 acres and several hundred feet of shoreline on Clear Lake in southwestern Sibley County. Picnicking and camping are the primary uses of the park.

Camping: Several campsites are situated along the lakeshore, with tables, fire rings, and vault toilets. A free camping permit is required for overnight camping.

Picnic Area: Facilities include two shelters, picnic tables, grills, a water pump, and vault toilets.

Water Recreation: A dirt boat ramp provides boating and fishing access to Clear Lake. It is also possible to swim from the park's shoreline.
Trails: None.
Recreational Facilities: Playground equipment is provided.
Seasons: The park is open from May through September.
Directions: From Gaylord, take State Highway 19 west for 12 miles, turn left and go south on County Road 3 for 5 miles, then turn right and go west on County Road 8 for 2 miles, following the park signs.

33. High Island Creek County Park

Two hundred acres of mixed hardwood forest and rolling terrain dominate the landscape of this park. The High Island Creek flows through here on its way to the Minnesota River.
Camping: None.
Picnic Area: A shelter, picnic tables, grills, a water pump, and vault toilets are provided.
Water Recreation: None.
Trails: The park doesn't have any developed trails; however, you can explore the park's forest on foot.
Recreational Facilities: None.
Seasons: The park is open from May through September.
Directions: From Gaylord, take State Highway 5 east for 7 miles, then County Road 12 east for 7.5 miles.

Swift County

Parks Department
Highway Department Building
1000 15th Street South
Benson, MN 56215
(320) 843-5341
www.swiftcounty.com

34. Appleton Area Off-Highway Vehicle Park

This is one of the more unique and specialized county parks in Minnesota. Once the site of Appleton Lake Park, it has now been converted into an off-highway vehicle (OHV) park with trails and scramble areas. This park is designed to meet the ever-increasing demand for areas to ride all-terrain vehicles and off-highway motorcycles.

Camping: None.

Picnic Area: A picnic shelter and picnic tables are provided at the parking lot.

Water Recreation: None.

Trails: Several miles of OHV trails wind through a mixed hardwood forest. This is a single-use park primarily designed for motorized recreation.

Recreational Facilities: None.

Seasons: The park is open during the nonwinter months. The actual opening and closing dates vary from April through September depending upon the trail conditions. Check the website or call the contact number for up-to-date information regarding whether the park is open or closed.

Directions: From Benson, take U.S. Highway 12 west for 16 miles to U.S. Highway 59, turn left and go south, then head southwest for 7 miles to the park entrance, which is 2 miles northeast of Appleton.

35. Swift Falls Park

Swift Falls Park is located in a small hollow along the East Branch of the Chippewa River in northeast Swift County. It offers visitors a quiet retreat for camping or picnicking near the historic village of Swift Falls. Once used as pastureland, this area was converted to a park in 1964.

Camping: The campground features four RV sites and four tent sites. The sites include tables and campfire rings. A handicap-accessible restroom and shower building is conveniently located in the middle of the campground and picnic area. A fee is charged for overnight camping.

Picnic Area: The picnic area features several picnic tables and grills and six shelters that are available for use.

Water Recreation: The East Branch of the Chippewa River offers fishing and wading opportunities in the park.

Trails: A series of short walking trails wind their way across bridges and along both sides of the river.

Recreational Facilities: Older-style playground equipment is provided.

Seasons: The park is open from May through September.

Directions: From Benson, take State Highway 9 east for 4.5 miles, take County Road 31 north for 6.5 miles to County Road 25; turn right (east) and go through the community of Swift Falls, then cross a bridge; the park entrance is on the right side of the road.

Wright County

County Parks Department
1901 Highway 25N
Buffalo, MN 55313
(763) 682-7693
www.co.wright.mn.us/department/parks.asp

36. Beebe Lake Regional Park

This is primarily a day-use park that provides opportunities for picnicking, swimming, boating, and overnight camping in a group camp area. The beach aand fishing areas are secluded from the parking lot by a thick strand of mixed hardwood trees.

Camping: A group camp is available for large family or organized groups. A fee is charged for use of the group camp, and a caretaker is on duty.

Picnic Area: A shelter, picnic tables, and handicap-accessible modern restrooms are provided. A fee is charged for picnic-shelter use.

Water Recreation: Beebe Lake offers fishing and boating opportunities. Facilities include a concrete ramp, a large swimming beach, and a fishing dock.

Beebe Lake Regional Park

Trails: A 1-mile-long hiking trail is provided.

Recreational Facilities: A creative playground structure and volleyball court is provided.

Seasons: The park is open from early May to late September.

Directions: From Buffalo, take County Road 34 east for 6 miles; the park entrance is on the left side of the road.

37. Carl Johnson County Forest

This 40-acre forest features ravines and a mixture of hardwood trees. A small picnic area and a short trail are the only developed facilities.

Camping: None.

Picnic Area: A small picnic area is provided.

Water Recreation: None.

Trails: Hikers can enjoy a short, 1-mile-long trail through the forest.

Recreational Facilities: None.

Seasons: The park is open year-round.

Directions: From Buffalo, take County Road 35 west for 15 miles, then follow the signs from County Road 35.

38. Clearwater/Pleasant Regional Park

This park is a preserve for about 210 acres of land between Clearwater and Pleasant Lakes in the northern part of Wright County. The developed picnic area and beach are located on Pleasant Lake.

Camping: None.

Picnic Area: Amenities include a shelter, picnic tables, and modern restrooms. A park caretaker is on duty during the day.

Water Recreation: Pleasant Lake features boating, fishing, and swimming activities. A large swimming beach and concrete boat ramp are provided.

Trails: Two miles of trails are provided in the park, and a paved trail connects the park to the city of Annandale.

Recreational Facilities: A modern play structure and volleyball courts are provided.

Seasons: The park is open from May through September.

Directions: From Buffalo, take State Highway 55 northwest for 15 miles to Annandale, then turn right and go north on State Highway 24 for 1 mile; the park entrance is on the left side of the road off Highway 24 and County Road 39.

39. Clearwater Wayside

Large oaks and red cedars highlight this small, six-acre wayside rest area near the town of Clearwater. The site provides a nice location for a picnic lunch or break when traveling.

Camping: None.

Picnic Area: Picnic tables and grills are located next to the parking lot and down the hill near the Clearwater River. A portable toilet is provided at the parking lot during the summer months.

Water Recreation: None.

Trails: None.

Recreational Facilities: None.

Seasons: The park is open year-round.

Directions: From Saint Cloud, go 10 miles southeast on Interstate 94 to State Highway 24 at the Clearwater exit; go north on State Highway 24 for a short distance, looking for County Road 75; then go west (left) on County Road 75 for a quarter mile. The wayside is on the left side of the road.

40. Collinwood Regional Park

This is a nice family park and campground located on Collinwood Lake. It includes a campground, picnic area, swimming beach, and hiking trails on over 300 acres.

Camping: Camping facilities include 49 RV/tent sites with electrical hookups, and there are handicap-accessible restrooms with showers. A fee is charged for overnight camping, and a resident caretaker lives on-site.

Picnic Area: A shelter, picnic tables, and toilets are provided.

Water Recreation: Collinwood Lake offers fishing and boating opportunities. Facilities include a nice, sandy swimming beach, a concrete ramp, and a handicap-accessible floating fishing pier.

Trails: Five miles of hiking/skiing trails are maintained.

Recreational Facilities: A creative playground structure is available for children.

Seasons: The campground is open from early May through September, while the trails are open year-round.

Directions: The park is located about 50 miles west of the Twin Cities. Take U.S. Highway 12 west to Rhoades Avenue, about 3 miles west of Cokato. Turn south and drive 2 miles to 70th Street SW, where the campground is located. A vehicle permit is required for entry into the park.

(To read more about the park, see "25 Favorite County Parks" in the first section of this guide.)

41. Dustin Monument Wayside

This is a small historic wayside area located on U.S. Highway 12 west of Howard Lake. It provides a nice area for a quick break from the road or a picnic lunch.

Camping: None.

Picnic Area: A shelter, picnic tables, and grills are provided.

Water Recreation: None.

Trails: None.

Recreational Facilities: None.

Seasons: The park is open year-round.

Directions: From Buffalo, take State Highway 25 south for 8 miles, then turn right and go west on U.S. Highway 12 for 19 miles to Rhoades Avenue, which is 3 miles west of Cokato. Turn south on Rhoades and drive 2 miles to 70th Street SW, where the campground is located.

42. Fairhaven Mill Historic Wayside

This is the site of a historic gristmill and spillway dam. The mill itself is not currently open to visitors. The site features picnicking, shore fishing, and lake access.

Camping: None.

Picnic Area: Picnic tables, grills, and a portable toilet are located next to the mill.

Water Recreation: A boat ramp provides boating and fishing access to Mill Pond. Fishing can also be enjoyed from the shoreline near the dam.

Trails: None.

Recreational Facilities: None.

Seasons: The park is open year-round.

Directions: From Buffalo, take State Highway 55 northwest for 20 miles to County Road 2 at South Haven, then turn right and go north on County Road 2 for 2 miles; the park entrance is on the left side of the road.

43. Harry Larson County Forest

The area features 170 acres of rolling forest and wetlands. It features trails and a small picnic area.

Camping: None.

Picnic Area: Facilities include a few picnic tables and vault toilets.

Water Recreation: None.

Trails: Two miles of hiking/skiing trails are provided.

Recreational Facilities: None.

Seasons: The park is open year-round.

Directions: From Buffalo, take State Highway 55 northwest for 7 miles to Maple Lake, turn right and go north on County Road 8 for 5 miles, then turn right and go east on County Road 39 for 4 miles; turn left and go north on County Road 111 for 1 mile. Watch for the park entrance on the right side of the road.

44. Marcus Zumbrunnen County Park

This small county park is located only a half mile from Interstate 94. It is a nice spot for a quick stop and stretch when traveling, but it doesn't provide any toilet or water facilities.

Camping: None.

Picnic Area: One picnic table is provided.

Water Recreation: None.

Trails: A short, 1-mile-long hiking trail winds through the mixed hardwood and pine forest of the park.

Recreational Facilities: None.

Seasons: The park is open year-round.

Directions: From Saint Cloud, go 15 miles southeast on Interstate 94 to County Road 8 at the Hasty exit and go south on County Road 8 for a half mile; the park is on the right side of the road.

45. Montissippi Regional Park

This quiet day-use park is located on the Mississippi River south of Saint Cloud. It offers an enjoyable location for picnicking, river fishing, or trail walking. A mixed hardwood forest and some pine plantations cover most of the park's 170 acres. The park's name appears to be derived from the combination of "Mont" (from the name of the nearest town, "Monticello") and "issippi" (from "Mississippi River").

Camping: None.

Picnic Area: A small picnic area occupies the gentle slope from the parking lot to the river. A few picnic tables, grills, and a portable toilet are provided.

Water Recreation: The Mississippi River provides fishing and boating opportunities. The park includes a ramp for boat or canoe access and a handicap-accessible floating fishing pier.

Trails: Two loops of paved hiking trails that total 2 miles in length are provided. These trails are also open for cross-country skiing in the winter. Opportunities include a short nature trail that explores and interprets the mixed hardwood forest.

Recreational Facilities: The park has a very nice modern play structure with several features for small children.

Seasons: The park is open year-round.

Directions: Take Interstate 94 northwest from the Twin Cities to the Monticello exit and State Highway 25; go north on Highway 25 a short distance to County Road 75, then go west on County Road 75 for 2 miles; the park entrance is on the right side of the road.

46. Mud Lake County Park

This is a small day-use park that features a picnic area and a boat ramp. It features scenic views of the lake and opportunities for fishing from shore.

Camping: None.

Picnic Area: Picnic tables, grills, and vault toilets are provided.

Water Recreation: Access to Mud Lake for boating and fishing is provided by a boat launch and a fishing dock.

Trails: None.

Recreational Facilities: None.

Seasons: The park is open from May through September.

Directions: From Buffalo, take County Road 35 west for 15 miles; the park entrance is on the left side of the road.

47. Oscar and Anna Johnson County Park

This is a small park located on Dog Lake in southern Wright County. It features a picnic area and comfortable swimming beach.

Camping: None.

Picnic Area: Picnic tables, grills, and vault toilets are provided.

Water Recreation: A nice swimming beach is open during the summer, and a concrete ramp next to the park provides boat access to the lake.

Trails: None.

Recreational Facilities: None.

Seasons: The park is open from May through September.

Directions: From Buffalo, take State Highway 25 south for 7 miles, turn right and go west on U.S. Highway 12 for 5 miles to County Road 8; take that south for 3 miles, then turn right and go west on County Road 30 for about 1.5 miles. Follow the park signs from County Road 30, heading south and west for 1.5 miles to the entrance.

48. Otsego Regional Park

Visitors can enjoy a quiet walk or a picnic in this 70-acre park. It features a mixed hardwood forest and prairie landscape along the Mississippi River.

Camping: None.

Picnic Area: Facilities include two shelters, picnic tables, and handicap-accessible restrooms.

Water Recreation: Shoreline fishing and canoe access to the Mississippi River is provided.

Trails: Two miles of paved trails wind through the park and offer hiking and biking opportunities.

Recreational Facilities: A handicap-accessible modern play structure and ball field is provided.

Seasons: The park is open from May through September.

Directions: From Buffalo, take County Road 34 east for 10 miles, turn left and take County Road 19 north for 10 miles to County Road 39; turn right and take that east for 5 miles, then turn left on County Road 42 in Elk River; be ready to turn left in less than a half mile and follow the signs to the park.

49. Robert Ney Memorial Park Reserve

This park reserve includes 650 acres of forest and wetlands that provide habitat for a variety of wildlife. The park also contains the Wright County Parks Environmental Education Center, which can be reserved for group activities.

Camping: None.

Picnic Area: Facilities include a few picnic tables, a memorial chapel, and a portable toilet.

Water Recreation: A boat ramp provides access to Lake Mary.

Trails: Three-and-a-half miles of hiking/skiing trails are provided.

Recreational Facilities: None.

Seasons: The park is open year-round.

Directions: From Buffalo, take State Highway 55 northwest for 7 miles to Maple Lake, then turn right and take County Road 8 north for 1.5 miles; follow the signs to the park.

50. Schroeder Regional Park

Schroeder is a popular park located on Cedar Lake near Annandale. It features camping, swimming, picnicking, and lake-access opportunities. The park is a popular destination and it is usually very busy during the summer.

Camping: Facilities include 50 RV/tent campsites with electrical hookups and handicap-accessible restrooms with showers. A fee is charged for overnight camping, and a resident caretaker lives on-site.

Picnic Area: Facilities include a shelter, picnic tables, and toilets.

Water Recreation: Cedar Lake offers fishing and boating opportunities. Facilities include a concrete ramp, a large swimming beach, and a handicap-accessible floating fishing pier. A fee is charged for using the boat ramp.

Trails: A short hiking trail provides an opportunity to stretch your legs.

Recreational Facilities: A creative playground structure and volleyball court is provided.

Seasons: The park is open from early May through September.

Directions: From Buffalo, take State Highway 55 northwest for 8 miles, turn right and go north on County Road 7 for 5 miles, then turn left and go west on County Road 39 for 1 mile. The park entrance is on the left side of the road.

51. Stanley Eddy Memorial Park Reserve

Covering nearly 660 acres, this park reserve preserves natural habitat, forest, and wetlands. A majority of the park is maintained in its natural condition, with the only development being a few miles of trails and a couple of picnic areas.

Camping: None.

Picnic Area: The northern and southern sections of the park include picnic sites with tables and vault toilets.

Water Recreation: None.

Trails: Nearly 8 miles of hiking/skiing trails are provided.

Recreational Facilities: None.

Seasons: The park is open year-round.

Directions: From Buffalo, take State Highway 25 south for 7 miles to U.S. Highway 12, turn right and go west for 16 miles to County Road 3 in Cakato; turn left on County Road 3 and go north for a few miles to the park entrance.

52. Stirewalt Memorial County Park

This facility is located on Limestone Lake in northern Wright County. It is a small day-use park that offers picnicking and fishing opportunities.

Camping: None.

Picnic Area: Tables are provided.

Water Recreation: Facilities include a fishing platform on Limestone Lake.

Trails: None.

Recreational Facilities: None.

Seasons: The park is open from May through September.

Directions: From Buffalo, take State Highway 55 northwest for 7 miles to Maple Lake, turn right and go north on County Road 8 for 9 miles; then follow the park signs from County Road 8 to the park.

Wright County features seven parks located along the north fork of the Crow River. These parks feature forested shoreline along the river and a variety of amenities.

53. Albright's Mill County River Park

Camping: One canoe campsite is provided in the park with a fire ring and a picnic table.

Picnic Area: Facilities include a couple of picnic tables, grills, and a pit toilet.

Water Recreation: Canoeing and fishing access is provided on the north fork of the Crow River.

Trails: None.

Recreational Facilities: None.

Seasons: The park is open from May through September.

Directions: From Buffalo, take County Road 35 west for 12 miles, then turn left and go south on County Road 5 for 2 miles.

54. Betty Mason County River Park

Camping: None.

Picnic Area: None.

Water Recreation: Canoeing and fishing access is provided on the north fork of the Crow River.

Trails: None.

Recreational Facilities: None.

Seasons: The park is open from May through September.

Directions: From Buffalo, take County Road 35 west for 16 miles, then turn left and go south on County Road 3 for a half mile.

55. Bill Anderson Memorial County River Park

Camping: Two water-access-only canoe campsites are provided in the park, along with fire rings, a picnic table, and pit toilets.

Picnic Area: Picnic tables and grills are provided.

Water Recreation: Canoeing and fishing access is provided on the north fork of the Crow River.
Trails: None.
Recreational Facilities: None.
Seasons: The park is open from May through September.
Directions: From Buffalo, take County Road 35 west for 7 miles, then turn left and go south on County Road 7 for 1.5 miles.

56. Crow Springs County River Park

Camping: One canoe campsite is provided in the park with a fire ring, a picnic table, and a nearby vault toilet.
Picnic Area: Amenities include a few picnic tables and grills and vault toilets.
Water Recreation: Canoeing and fishing access is provided on the north fork of the Crow River.
Trails: None.
Recreational Facilities: None.
Seasons: The park is open from May through September.
Directions: From Buffalo, take State Highway 25 south for 6 miles; the park entrance is on the right side of the road.

57. Humphrey Arends County River Park

Camping: One canoe campsite is provided in the park with a fire ring and a picnic table.
Picnic Area: Facilities include a couple of picnic tables, grills, and pit toilets.
Water Recreation: Canoeing and fishing access is provided on the north fork of the Crow River.
Trails: None.
Recreational Facilities: None.
Seasons: The park is open from May through September.
Directions: From Buffalo, take County Road 35 west for 4 miles, then turn left and go south on County Road 9 for 4 miles.

58. Riverside County River Park

Camping: One canoe campsite is provided in the park with a fire ring and a picnic table.
Picnic Area: Facilities include a couple of picnic tables, grills, and vault toilets.
Water Recreation: Canoeing and fishing access is provided on the Crow River.

Trails: None.

Recreational Facilities: None.

Seasons: The park is open from May through September.

Directions: From Buffalo, take County Road 34 east for 10 miles to Hanover, turn left on River Road NE, then turn right on 8th Street NE and follow it to the end (gravel).

59. Wildlife County River Park

Camping: Two canoe campsites are provided in the park with a fire ring, a picnic table, and a nearby vault toilet.

Picnic Area: One picnic table is provided.

Water Recreation: Canoeing and fishing access is provided on the north fork of the Crow River.

Trails: None.

Recreational Facilities: None.

Seasons: The park is open from May through September.

Directions: From Buffalo, take County Road 35 west for 16 miles, turn left and go south on County Road 3 for 1 mile; follow the park signs from County Road 3.

Yellow Medicine County

Highway Department
415 8th Avenue
Granite Falls, MN 56241
(320) 564-3331

60. Oraas County Park

This is a nice wayside park located in central Yellow Medicine County. It features a mixed hardwood forest, a picnic area, and dispersed camping.

Camping: Beyond the parking area, camping is allowed within the park at undesignated sites. There are a few fire rings and picnic tables provided. A handicap-accessible vault toilet is located near the parking area.

Picnic Area: A small shelter and a few picnic tables are provided.

Water Recreation: None.

Trails: A short hiking trail is provided that winds through the forest.

Recreational Facilities: None.

Seasons: The park is open year-round.

Directions: From Granite Falls, take State Highway 23 southwest for 6.5 miles to County Road 18 in Hanley Falls; turn right and take County Road 18 west for 6.5 miles, then turn left on Highway 59; the park will be immediately on the right side of the road.

61. Timm County Park

Located on Wood Lake, this park offers camping, picnicking, and water activities. It features a hardwood forest and rolling hills landscape, and the campground overlooks the lake.

Camping: The campground includes 12 RV/tent sites and vault toilets. Camping is first-come, first-served and no fees are charged.

Picnic Area: A small picnic area alongside the lake includes a shelter, picnic tables, and grills.

Water Recreation: A concrete boat ramp provides boating and fishing access to Wood Lake.

Trails: None.

Recreational Facilities: None.

Seasons: The park is open from May through September.

Directions: From Granite Falls, take State Highway 23 south for 2 miles to State Highway 274; take that south for 3.5 miles, then turn left at County Road 18 and take it east for a half mile; then turn right on 557th Street.

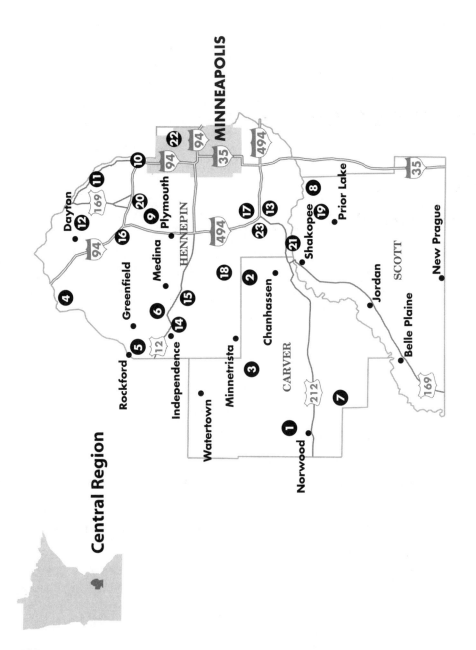

Central Region

MINNEAPOLIS

CENTRAL REGION

Parks Office
11360 Highway 212 West
PO Box 330
Cologne, MN 55322
(952) 466-5250
www.co.carver.mn.us/parks

1. Baylor Regional Park

Located on Eagle Lake, Baylor Park features 200 acres of forests, fields, lakeshore, and wetlands to enjoy and explore. Facilities include a campground, picnic area, beach, and a restored 1935 barn that can be reserved for parties or special events.

Camping: The campground features 35 modern campsites with water and electrical hookups and 15 primitive campsites with no hookups. Additional facilities include handicap-accessible restrooms and showers and an RV dump station. A fee is charged for overnight camping, and park caretakers live on-site.

Picnic Area: Two picnic shelters and several picnic tables and grills are provided. One shelter overlooks the wetlands, while the other is near the beach.

Water Recreation: Eagle Lake offers boating, fishing, and swimming opportunities. A large, sandy beach provides hours of swimming fun, while boaters can access the lake from a nearby boat ramp. Paddleboat rentals are also available from the park during the summer.

Trails: Five miles of hiking and skiing trails wind their way through maple trees, open fields, and the wetlands of the park. The wetland boardwalk makes a unique hiking and skiing trail, and snowshoe rentals are available during the winter.

Recreational Facilities: Other facilities include two modern playgrounds, tennis courts, volleyball courts, and ball fields.

Seasons: The park is open year-round for day use, and the campground is open from mid-May through mid-October.

Directions: From Norwood Young America, take County Road 33 north for

2.5 miles; the park entrance is on the right side of the road. An annual vehicle permit is required for entry.

2. Lake Minnewashta Regional Park

Over 300 acres of forest, fields, and wetlands on Lake Minnewashta await visitors to this park. Picnicking and lake access seem to be the most popular recreational opportunities enjoyed by visitors.

Camping: None.

Picnic Area: Two picnic areas, four picnic shelters with electricity, picnic tables, grills, and restroom facilities are provided.

Water Recreation: Lake Minnewashta offers boating, fishing, and swimming opportunities. Within the park, a sandy swimming beach, two boat ramps, and a handicap-accessible fishing pier are provided. A concessions building is located next to the beach.

Trails: Five miles of hiking and skiing trails wind their way through the forests and fields of the park.

Recreational Facilities: A modern creative play structure is provided near the picnic shelters.

Seasons: The park is open year-round for trail and lake access.

Directions: From Norwood Young America, take State Highway 5 northeast for 18 miles to State Highway 41; turn left and go north for 1 mile. An annual vehicle permit is required for entry into the park.

3. Lake Waconia Regional Park

A local favorite for picnics and swimming, this small park features a sandy beach and a grassy picnic area. Travelers along Highway 5 can also enjoy this park as a rest stop.

Camping: None.

Picnic Area: A large picnic shelter, picnic tables, grills, and a handicap-accessible portable toilet are provided.

Water Recreation: Swimmers can enjoy a sandy beach on Lake Waconia that is supervised by lifeguards during the summer months.

Trails: None.

Recreational Facilities: Older-style playground equipment is provided.

Seasons: The park is open from May through September.

Directions: From Norwood Young America, take State Highway 5 northeast 8.5 miles to the park, which is on the left side of the road.

Hennepin County

Hennepin County parks are administered by the Three Rivers Park District.

Scott County

Scott County parks are administered by the Three Rivers Park District.

Three Rivers Park District

Administration Center
3000 Xenium Lane North
Plymouth, MN 55441
(763) 559-9000 (office)
(763) 559-6700 (reservations)
www.threeriversparkdistrict.org

Three Rivers is the only park district in Minnesota. It was established in 1957 to create a system of regional parks, trails, and preserves for the protection of natural resources and the enjoyment of residents in the Twin Cities metropolitan area and the state. The district operates with an elected board of commissioners separate from the county boards. Currently, the district owns 27,000 acres of parkland in six counties.

4. Crow-Hassan Park Reserve

Crow-Hassan Park Reserve is nearly 2,600 acres in size and preserves a landscape of hardwood forest, prairie, and prairie pothole ponds in northwestern Hennepin County. The large system of trails, used for a variety of recreational activities, is probably the most popular aspect of this park.

Camping: Three group camps are available by reservation.

Picnic Area: Several picnic tables, a water pump, and vault toilets are provided at the trailhead parking lot.

Water Recreation: None.

Trails: There are 13 miles of hiking trails, 9 miles of horse and pet trails, 5 miles of snowmobile trails, and 2 miles of snowshoe trails within the park.

Recreational Facilities: None.

Seasons: The park is open year-round, and a warming shelter is provided during the winter.

Directions: From the junction of Interstates 494 and 94, take I-94 northwest for 9 miles to the Rogers exit, turn left to go south through Rogers, then turn right and go northwest on County Road 116 for 3 miles; turn left and go west on Park Road 203 for about 2 miles. An annual vehicle permit is required for entry into the park.

5. Lake Rebecca Park Reserve

Trails, trees, and small lakes cover this park's 2,500 acres. The developed-use area is concentrated on the north end of Lake Rebecca and features extensive picnic and lake access areas. The motor restriction on Lake Rebecca makes this a nice place to enjoy a quiet canoeing or kayaking experience.

Camping: Two group camps are available by reservation.

Picnic Area: Four large reservation-only picnic areas and one general picnic area include picnic tables, grills, and handicap-accessible toilets. Three reservation-only areas include large shelters.

Rent a canoe at Lake Rebecca Park Reserve.

Water Recreation: A large swimming beach, two fishing piers, and a concrete boat ramp are provided. Only electric motors are allowed on Lake Rebecca. The park operates a canoe, boat, and paddleboat rental concession.

Trails: Trail users will enjoy 7 miles of paved biking/hiking trails, 9 miles of horse/pet trails, and 3.50 miles of mountain-biking trails.

Recreational Facilities: A modern play structure is located near the beach and general picnic area. The park includes a 30-acre pet exercise area.

Seasons: The park is open year-round.

Directions: From Plymouth, take State Highway 55 west for 15 miles to County Road 50, then turn left and go southwest on County Road 50 for 1.5 miles. An annual vehicle permit is required for entry into the park.

6. Baker Park Reserve

"A little bit of something for everybody" is the best way to describe this park. Four lakes, several wetlands, meadows, and a hardwood forest characterize the landscape. Numerous trails, several picnic areas, a large beach, rustic cabins, a

Baker Park Reserve features lakes, trails, and a golf course.

golf course, and the largest developed campground in the Three Rivers Park District system are provided.

Camping: There are 210 RV/tent sites, of which 98 include electricity, paved roads, an RV dump station, and handicap-accessible restrooms with showers. A fee is charged for overnight camping, and reservations can be made in advance. A vehicle permit is also needed for entry into the park. There are also five reservation-only group camps spread throughout the park.

Picnic Area: Four large reservation-only picnic areas and two general picnic areas include picnic tables, grills, and nearby handicap-accessible toilets. Three reservation-only picnic areas include large shelters.

Water Recreation: An unguarded swimming beach, two fishing piers, and a concrete boat ramp are provided on Lake Independence. Fishing piers are also provided on Half Moon and Spurzem Lakes. Half Moon Lake has a canoe carry-in access, and Spurzem Lake has a dirt boat ramp. A canoe, kayak, rowboat, and paddleboat rental concession is located adjacent to the swimming beach and picnic area on Lake Independence.

Trails: Seven miles of paved biking/hiking trails, 9 miles of horse/pet trails, and 2.5 miles of hiking-only trails are provided.

Recreational Facilities: A modern play structure is located near the beach and general picnic area. The Baker National Golf Course features 27 holes of championship golf. The near-wilderness settlement features rustic cabins available for group use.

Seasons: The park is open year-round for trail use; the campground is open from May through September.

Directions: From Plymouth, take State Highway 55 west for 9 miles, then turn left and go south on County Road 19 for 3 miles. An annual vehicle permit is required for entry into the park.

7. Carver Park Reserve

The 3,300 acres that make up this park include 10 lakes and a variety of habitats, which makes it a popular location for wildlife and nature observation. The Lowry Nature Center is located in the center of the park and features a variety of nature-oriented programs for kids, adults, and families.

Camping: The Lake Auburn Family Campground has 56 RV/tent sites, an RV dump station, and handicap-accessible vault toilets. A fee is charged for overnight camping, and reservations can be made in advance. In addition, there are four reservation-only group camps in other parts of the park.

Picnic Area: A reservation-only picnic area is located near Parley Lake and includes picnic tables, grills, and vault toilets.

Water Recreation: Canoeing, kayaking, and small boating can be enjoyed on three of the larger lakes. A swimming beach and fishing pier is located next to the campground on Lake Auburn. Steiger and Auburn Lakes feature dirt boat ramps and fishing piers, and a dirt boat ramp is also provided on Lake Zumbra.

Trails: Eight miles of paved biking/hiking trails, 3 miles of pet trails, and 12 miles of hiking-only trails are provided.

Recreational Facilities: The Lowry Nature Center features a unique habitat play area, featuring structures like larger-than-life flowers and a kid-sized beaver lodge.

Seasons: The park is open year-round for trail and nature center use, and the campground is open from May through September.

Directions: From Plymouth, take Interstate 494 south for 11 miles to State Highway 5, go west on Highway 5 for 10 miles, turn right and head north on County Road 11 for a short distance. An annual vehicle permit is required for entry into the park.

8. Murphy-Hanrehan Park Reserve

A relatively undeveloped park, Murphy-Hanrehan Park Reserve offers quiet trail experiences on 2,700 acres of rolling forest in Scott County. Mountain biking and horseback riding seem to be the most popular activities.

Camping: None.

Picnic Area: None.

Water Recreation: The Murphy and Hanrehan Lakes are small, but they provide fishing opportunities. A dirt ramp provides access to Murphy Lake.

Trails: There are 14 miles of hiking trails, 13 miles of horse trails, 6 miles of mountain-biking trails, 3 miles of pet trails, 12 miles of ski trails, 6 miles of dogsled trails, 4 miles of snowmobile trails, and 6 miles of snowshoe trails within the park. A handicap-accessible vault toilet is provided at the parking area.

Recreational Facilities: None.

Seasons: The park is open year-round.

Directions: From Plymouth, take Interstate 494 east to Interstate 35, take I-35 for 8 miles south, then turn right and take County Road 42 for 4 miles west; turn left and go south on County Road 27 for 2 miles, then turn left and go east on 154th Street for 1 mile; turn right and go south on County Road 75. An annual vehicle permit is required for entry into the park.

9. Clifton E. French Regional Park

Located on Medicine Lake in Plymouth, Clifton F. French Regional Park offers opportunities that include trails, picnic areas, and water access. It is also the location of the park district's headquarters, which includes a very nice visitor center with meeting rooms and a concession operation.

Camping: None.

Picnic Area: Facilities include a general picnic area near the beach, two reservation-only picnic areas with shelters, one reservation-only area without a shelter, picnic tables, grills, and handicap-accessible restrooms.

Water Recreation: Fishing, canoeing, kayaking, sailing, and boating can be enjoyed on Medicine Lake. A swimming beach and boat ramp are located adjacent to each other on the south end of the park.

Trails: Three miles of paved biking/hiking trails, 4 miles of pet trails, 6 miles of skiing trails, and 3 miles of hiking-only trails are provided.

Recreational Facilities: A very large, creative play structure is located next to the visitor center.

Seasons: The park is open year-round for trail and visitor center use.

Directions: From Plymouth, go east on County Road 9 for 2 miles, passing Interstate 494 on the way. An annual vehicle permit is required for entry into the park.

10. North Mississippi Regional Park

Located between Interstate 94 and the Mississippi River, this park offers visitors the opportunity to experience a natural Mississippi River shoreline only minutes north of Minneapolis. A large visitor center is open to assist visitors and to support nature interpretation and education activities.

Camping: None.

Picnic Area: Facilities include a large shelter, picnic tables, grills, and handicap-accessible restrooms.

Water Recreation: Shoreline fishing on the banks of the Mississippi can be enjoyed in the park.

Trails: Two miles of paved, handicap-accessible biking/hiking trails are provided.

Recreational Facilities: A large, creative play structure is located next to the large picnic shelter.

Seasons: The park and visitor center is open year-round.

Directions: From Interstate 94, take either the 49th or 53rd street exits for access to the visitor center and picnic area.

North Mississippi Regional Park

11. Coon Rapids Dam Regional Park

This Mississippi riverfront park is located directly across from a sister park with the same name in Anoka County. Together they preserve the shoreline above and below the Coon Rapids spillway dam.

Camping: None.

Picnic Area: A visitor center, picnic shelter, picnic tables, and restrooms are provided.

Water Recreation: Shoreline fishing on the banks of the Mississippi can be enjoyed from various locations within the park. The most popular is just below the dam. A handicap-accessible fishing deck is located next to the dam.

Trails: Two miles of paved, handicap-accessible biking/hiking trails, 2.50 miles of hiking/pet trails, and 2 miles of snowshoe trails are provided.

Recreational Facilities: None.

Seasons: The park and visitor center is open year-round.

Directions: On the west side of the Mississippi River in Brooklyn Park, take State Highway 610 to the Noble Parkway exit, turn north and go a short distance to 97th Avenue, turn east and take that to Russell Avenue (County Road 12); then turn north. An annual vehicle permit is required for entry into the park.

12. Elm Creek Park Reserve

Elm Creek Park Reserve is the largest park in the Three Rivers system. It offers a variety of developed recreation areas and vast expanses of natural areas to enjoy on over 5,000 acres. It is also home to the Eastman Nature Center, which hosts a variety of nature and outdoor programs throughout the year.

Camping: Two group camps are available and can be reserved for groups of 35 to 50 people. A third group camp is available for horse riders.

Picnic Area: Facilities include four reservation-only picnic areas and two general picnic areas. Three of the reservation-only areas have shelters, numerous picnic tables, grills, and toilets. Concessions and equipment rentals are provided near the swimming beach and picnic areas.

Water Recreation: There are five small lakes within the park that have been kept in a natural condition. No direct access is provided to these lakes. Swimming opportunities are provided at a swimming pond that is chlorinated.

Trails: There are numerous trail opportunities at Elm Creek. A good place to start is at the visitor's center, which has concessions, equipment rental, and handicap-accessible restrooms. There are 15 miles of trails available for hiking, nearly 20 miles of paved biking/hiking trails, 5 miles of trails for mountain biking, nearly 18 miles of horse trails, and 5 miles of pet trails. During the winter the park features a tubing hill with snowmaking, a lighted beginners' downhill ski area with snowmaking, 6 miles of lighted ski trail, 2.50 miles of ski trails that have snowmaking, and an additional 12 miles of cross-country skiing trails.

Recreational Facilities: Facilities include horseshoes and volleyball, available near the picnic areas; a creative play structure located near the swimming area; a 30-acre pet exercise area; and an archery range.

Seasons: The park is open year-round.

Directions: From Plymouth, take U.S. Highway 169 north for 6 miles, turn left onto State Highway 81 and go northwest for 3 miles; then turn right on Territorial Road and watch for the park's main entrance. An annual vehicle permit is required for entry into the park.

(To read more about the park, see "25 Favorite COunty Parks" in the first section of this guide.)

13. Hyland Lake Park Reserve

Hyland Lake Park Reserve offers some of the most diverse recreational opportunities found in any one park. Visitors can enjoy golf, swimming, nature study, downhill skiing, snowshoeing, and picnicking, all on 1,000 acres. It is also home to the Richardson Nature Center, which hosts a variety of nature and outdoor programs throughout the year.

Camping: Group camps are available and can be reserved for groups of 35 to 50 people.

Picnic Area: Facilities include four reservation-only picnic areas (two with shelters), two general picnic areas, picnic tables, grills, and handicap-acce-ssible restrooms.

Water Recreation: Fishing, canoeing, swimming, and boating opportunities can be enjoyed on Bush and Hyland lakes. A swimming beach and boat ramp are provided on Bush Lake, while a handicap-accessible fishing pier, small boat and canoe rental concession, and visitor center are located on Hyland Lake.

Trails: Facilities include 6 miles of paved biking/hiking trails, 3 miles of pet trails, 7 miles of hiking trails, and 7 miles of winter skiing trails, some of them lighted.

Recreational Facilities: A creative play structure is provided near the picnic areas. A golf driving range, practice putting green, downhill ski and snowboard area, and ski jump are located in the northern part of the park.

Seasons: The park is open year-round.

Directions: From Plymouth, take Interstate 494 south and east for 12 miles, take Highway 169 south for a half mile, turn left and go east on Highwood Drive; watch for the park signs. An annual vehicle permit is required for entry into the park.

14. Gale Woods Farm

Rural farm life is preserved and celebrated in the metropolitan area at Gale Woods Farm. This farm features fully operational facilities, including crops and livestock designed to promote land stewardship and educational programs about agriculture and farming.

Camping: None.

Picnic Area: Picnic tables and grills are provided in the picnic area. A reservation-only picnic pavilion can accommodate up to 400 people.

Water Recreation: A handicap-accessible fishing pier and carry-in boat access provide fishing and boat access to Whaletail Lake.

Trails: A short hiking trail to the lake and a 3-mile-long hiking trail around the park is provided. A large replica of a red barn houses the animals, farm education programs, and handicap-accessible restrooms. During the winter, the hiking trail is used for snowshoeing.

Recreational Facilities: None.

Seasons: The Gale Woods Farm is open year-round.

Directions: From Plymouth, take Interstate 494 south for 3 miles, take U.S. Highway 12 west for 13 miles to County Road 92; turn left and go south for 9 miles, then take County Road 110 east for 3 miles.

(To read more about the park, see "25 Favorite County Parks" in the first section of this guide.)

15. Noerenberg Memorial Park

Located on the shores of Lake Minnetonka, this site was once the estate of Grain Belt Brewery founder Frederick Noerenberg. The estate was donated to the park district in 1972 to be preserved and maintained for the public's enjoyment. The gardens contain a wonderful array of annuals and perennials and still feature a couple of historic buildings from the original estate.

Camping: None.

Picnic Area: None.

Water Recreation: Scenic views of Lake Minnetonka can be enjoyed from within the park.

Trails: Handicap-accessible paths provide access for viewing the arboretum of flowers, shrubs, plants, and trees.

Recreational Facilities: The gardens are a very popular location for outdoor weddings; these events can be arranged by contacting the park district for reservations.

Seasons: The gardens are open from May 1 through October 15 each year.

Directions: From Plymouth, take Interstate 494 south for 3 miles, take U.S. Highway 12 west for 3 miles to County Road 15; continue west on County Road 15 for 3 miles to County Road 51; turn east and go 1 mile.

16. Fish Lake Regional Park

This day-use park offers picnicking, trails, and water-recreation opportunities on Fish Lake in Maple Grove. It also provides a nice rest stop when traveling through the area on Interstate 494.

Camping: None.

Picnic Area: Facilities include two general picnic areas, one reservation-only picnic area, one reservation-only pavilion near the beach, picnic tables, grills, and restrooms.

Water Recreation: Fishing, canoeing, swimming, and boating opportunities can be enjoyed on Fish Lake. A swimming beach, boat ramp, and handicap-accessible fishing pier provide access to the lake. Small boats and canoes can be rented in the park.

Trails: A 1-mile-long, paved, handicap-accessible biking/hiking trail, 2 miles of pet trails, 4 miles of hiking trails, and 2 miles of snowshoe trails are provided.

Recreational Facilities: None.

Seasons: The park is open year-round.

Directions: From Plymouth, take Interstate 494 north for 3 miles to the Bass Lake Road exit and go west on County Road 10 for 1 mile. An annual vehicle permit is required for entry into the park.

17. Bryant Lake Regional Park

Located on a small slope, this park overlooks Bryant Lake in Eden Prairie. It contains a large Frisbee-disc golf course and also offers picnicking, trails, swimming, and boating opportunities.

Camping: None.

Picnic Area: Facilities include two picnic areas that require reservations on weekends, one reservation-only pavilion, one general picnic area, picnic tables, grills, restrooms, and a concession stand.

Water Recreation: Fishing, canoeing, swimming, and boating opportunities can be enjoyed on Bryant Lake. A swimming beach, boat ramp, and handicap-accessible fishing pier provide access to the lake. Small boats and canoes can be rented in the park.

Trails: Two miles of paved, handicap-accessible biking/hiking trails, 2 miles of pet trails, and 1 mile of hiking/snowshoeing trails are provided.

Recreational Facilities: A creative play structure is provided.

Seasons: The park is open year-round.

Directions: From Plymouth, take Interstate 494 south for 8 miles to State Highway 62; go east on Highway 62 for 1 mile, then turn right and go south on Shady Oak Road; turn right and go west a short distance on Rowland Road. An annual vehicle permit is required for entry into the park.

18. Lake Minnetonka Regional Park

Visitors can start by exploring this park's unique visitor center to learn about the history of Lake Minnetonka. A boat ramp provides access to the lake near the visitor center. It also features a large, constructed swimming pond with a dandy beach surrounding it.

Lake Minnetonka Regional Park features a unique Visitor's Center.

Camping: None.

Picnic Area: Facilities include three general picnic areas, one reservation-only picnic area, picnic tables, grills, and handicap-accessible restrooms.

Water Recreation: A large, chlorinated swimming pond surrounded by sand and watched by lifeguards provides a safe and enjoyable swimming experience. A concrete boat ramp and handicap-accessible fishing pier provides access to the lake.

Trails: Trail users can enjoy 2.5 miles of paved biking/hiking trails, 1 mile of pet trail, 1 mile of hiking trails, and 2 miles of snowshoe trails.

Recreational Facilities: A large creative play structure is provided near the picnic areas.

Seasons: The park is open year-round.

Directions: From Plymouth, take Interstate 494 south for 6 miles, then go southwest on State Highway 7 for 12 miles. An annual vehicle permit is required for entry into the park.

19. Cleary Lake Regional Park

The boundary of this park completely encompasses Cleary Lake and provides a variety of water-oriented recreation activities for visitors in eastern Scott County. Bicycle riders and walkers can take the paved trail all the way around the lake, while campers can enjoy one of four group camp areas.

Camping: Five reservation-only group camps and one family campground provide unique opportunities for camping. One of the group camps is located on an island out in the lake.

Picnic Area: Facilities include one general picnic area, two reservation-only picnic areas, one reservation-only pavilion, picnic tables, grills, and handicap-accessible restrooms.

Water Recreation: Fishing, canoeing, swimming, and boating opportunities can be enjoyed on Cleary Lake. A swimming beach, dirt boat ramp, and handicap-accessible fishing pier provide access to the lake. Small boats and canoes can be rented in the park.

Trails: Trail users will find 3.50 miles of paved biking/hiking trails, 1 mile of pet trails, 4 miles of hiking trails, and 10 miles of winter skiing trails, some of them lighted.

Recreational Facilities: A nine-hole golf course and driving range are provided. The golf clubhouse also doubles as the park's visitor center. A creative play structure is located near the beach.

Seasons: The park is open year-round.

Directions: From Plymouth, take Interstate 494 south and east for 17 miles to Interstate 35W, take I-35W south for 7 miles to County Road 42; take County Road 42 west for 3 miles, then take County Road 27 south for 4 miles. An annual vehicle permit is required for entry into the park.

20. Eagle Lake Regional Park

With over 200 acres of land, Eagle Lake is primarily designed as a golf center with a few trails. The golf center features a small golf course and a variety of practice activities.

Camping: None.

Picnic Area: A reservation-only picnic shelter with picnic tables and restrooms is available year-round for large group use.

Water Recreation: None.

Trails: One mile of paved biking/hiking trails, 8 miles of skiing trails, and 1.5 miles of snowshoe trails are provided.

Recreational Facilities: The golf center includes a 9-hole regular golf course, a 9-hole lighted pitch-and-putt course, a 40-station, lighted, natural-turf practice range, and practice/lesson areas. A combination visitor center and clubhouse features a concession operation and a golf shop.

Seasons: The reservation-only shelter and trails are open year-round. The golf facilities are open from March through August.

Directions: From Plymouth, take Interstate 494 north for 3 miles, then take County Road 10 (Bass Lake Road) east for 2 miles.

21. Historic Murphy's Landing

The rich history of Minnesota comes alive at Historic Murphy's Landing. Life from 1840 to 1890 in the Minnesota River valley is enacted by costumed individuals, providing a fun and educational experience for school groups and families.

Camping: None.

Picnic Area: A pavilion and other sites can be reserved for large group events like weddings.

Water Recreation: None.

Trails: Visitors can walk among 40 historical buildings and real-life costumed interpreters who portray life during the historical period.

Recreational Facilities: None.

Seasons: Murphy's Landing is open on weekends from Memorial Day through mid-October and Thanksgiving through December each year. Admission fees are charged for entry into the park.

Directions: From Plymouth, take Interstate 494 south and east for 12 miles, then take U.S. Highway 169 south for 6 miles to State Highway 101; take that west for 4 miles.

22. Silverwood Park

Located on Silver Lake in Saint Anthony, this is the park district's newest park. It features 120 acres of a former camp and conference center on the shores of Silver Lake. While still under development, it is open for day use.

Camping: None.

Picnic Area: A shelter, picnic tables, and toilets are provided.

Water Recreation: Shoreline fishing and carry-in canoe or kayak access is permitted within the park. Silver Lake contains a variety of fish.

Trails: A 1-mile-long hiking trail is provided.

Recreational Facilities: None.

Seasons: Current park facilities are designed for use from May through September.

Directions: From Plymouth, take Interstate 494 south and east for 17 miles to Interstate 35W, take I-35W north for 15 miles, then take County Road 19 west for 2 miles.

23. Glen Lake Golf and Practice Center

Glen Lake Golf and Practice Center is primarily designed as a golf center. It features a nine-hole golf course and practice center located on 60 acres in Minnetonka.

Camping: None.

Picnic Area: None.

Water Recreation: None.

Trails: None.

Recreational Facilities: A nine-hole golf course, driving range, and lesson tees are provided.

Seasons: The golf facilities are open from March through August.

Directions: From Plymouth, take Interstate 494 south for 8 miles to County Road 62, then go west for 1 mile on County Road 62.

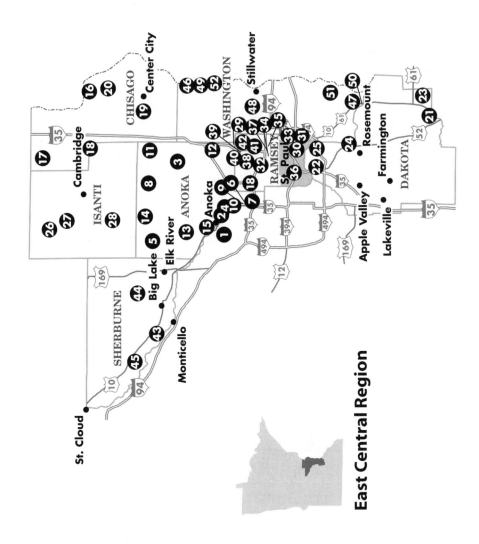

East Central Region

EAST-CENTRAL REGION

Anoka County

Parks and Recreation Department
550 Bunker Lake Blvd. NW
Anoka, MN 55304
(763) 757-3920
www.anokacountyparks.com

1. Anoka County Riverfront Regional Park

This park preserves the Riedel Farm Estate, which was built in the 1880s along a stretch of the Mississippi River on nearly 140 acres of land. The farmhouse has been restored and can be rented for special group events. A boat ramp, picnic areas, and trails are also commonly used facilities.

Camping: None.

Picnic Area: Facilities include two picnic pavilions with electricity, picnic tables, grills, and handicap-accessible restrooms.

Water Recreation: A concrete ramp provides boat/canoe and fishing access to the Mississippi River.

Trails: Two miles of paved biking/hiking trails run parallel to the river in the park. The trails are connected to the Mississippi River Regional Trail, which is a paved trail that runs along the river from Coon Rapids Dam Regional Park in the north to Anoka County Riverfront Regional Park in the south, connecting the Minneapolis Park System trails.

Recreational Facilities: Playground equipment is provided.

Seasons: The park is open year-round.

Directions: From Anoka, take County Road 1 south for 8.5 miles; watch for the park signs. A vehicle permit is required in the park.

2. Bunker Hills Regional Park

Bunker Hills features 1,600 acres of parkland with a wide variety of recreational opportunities. Visitors can choose from activities like golfing, hiking, horseback riding, picnicking, camping, or an outdoor water park. The Anoka County Parks and Recreation Department Office is also located in the park.

Camping: A large and comfortable campground features 27 RV sites with water and electrical hookups, 24 rustic tent/RV sites with vegetative screening between sites, a 30-person group campsite, two handicap-accessible restroom buildings with showers, and an RV dump station. Campground hosts live on-site, and a fee is charged for overnight camping.

Picnic Area: The picnic area features pavilions, picnic tables, grills, and restrooms in a wooded setting.

Water Recreation: Bunker Beach is a large, modern water park located in the park. A separate fee is charged for admission to the water park.

Trails: Visitors can enjoy 6 miles of paved biking/hiking trails, 4 miles of horse trails, 4 miles of hiking-only trails, and 15 kilometers of ski trails. The Bunker Park Stables offer trail rides, lessons, sleigh rides, and other special events at the stables and arena. Separate fees apply to activities at the stables.

Recreational Facilities: Additional activities include an outdoor and indoor archery range and the Bunker Hills Golf Course, which features 27 challenging holes of golf.

Seasons: The park is open year-round.

Directions: From Anoka, take State Highway 242 east for 4 miles; the park entrance is on the left side of the road. A vehicle permit is required in the park. *(To read more about the park, see "25 Favorite County Parks" in the first section of this guide.)*

3. Coon Lake County Park

Picnic and swimming opportunities exist at this quiet park, which is located on Coon Lake in northeastern Anoka County. A majority of the landscape has been kept in a natural condition.

Camping: None.

Picnic Area: The picnic area features two pavilions with electricity, several picnic tables, and restrooms.

Water Recreation: Swimming, boating, and fishing access is provided by a sand beach and boat/canoe ramp.

Trails: Hiking trails wind throughout the park's forested landscape.

Recreational Facilities: Playground equipment is provided near the beach.

Seasons: The park is open year-round.

Directions: From Anoka take State Highway 242 east for 5 miles, then turn left and go north on County Road 17 for 10 miles.

Coon Rapids Dam Regional Park

4. Coon Rapids Dam Regional Park

This park features the Coon Rapids Dam and a variety of recreational activities along the riverfront of the Mississippi. The dam was built in 1914 and renovated in 1997. The park's visitor center contains interpretive information about the river and the history of the dam.

The Three Rivers Park District operates a sister regional park with the same name on the opposite side of the dam.

Camping: None.

Picnic Area: Facilities include six shelters, family picnic areas, numerous picnic tables and grills, and handicap-accessible restrooms.

Water Recreation: Boating, canoeing, and fishing are possible in the park. Facilities include a boat/canoe launch on the Mississippi River, shoreline fishing, and a fishing pier on Cenaiko Trout Lake.

Trails: Visitors can enjoy 3 miles of paved biking/hiking trails and 3 miles of ski trails. Bicycles can be rented at the visitor center. The trails are connected to the Mississippi River Regional Trail, a paved path that runs along the river from Anoka in the north to the Anoka County Riverfront Regional Park in the south. Bike riders can also connect to the North Hennepin Trail Corridor by crossing the dam.

Recreational Facilities: A modern play structure is located near the trout lake, and a large performance pavilion hosts outdoor concerts during the summer.
Seasons: The park is open year-round.
Directions: From Anoka, take County Road 1 southeast for 3 miles (it turns into Coon Rapids Boulevard), then turn right and take Egret Boulevard south for 1 mile. A vehicle permit is required in the park.

5. East Twin Lake County Park

A large sandy beach provides cool relief for swimmers on hot summer days in this day-use park, which is located in western Anoka County. A picnic area, trails, and a boat ramp are also provided.
Camping: None.
Picnic Area: Facilities include two small shelters, picnic tables, grills, and handicap-accessible restrooms.
Water Recreation: Visitors can boat, fish, or swim in the waters of East Twin Lake. A sandy swimming beach, fishing pier, and dirt boat/canoe access are provided.
Trails: A few hiking trails are provided.
Recreational Facilities: Older-style playground equipment is located near the picnic area and beach.

Boat, picnic, or swim at East Twin Lake County Park.

Seasons: The park is open year-round.

Directions: From Anoka, take State Highway 47 north for 8 miles, turn left on County Road 22, and go west for 4 miles.

6. Islands of Peace County Park

Two islands and adjacent shoreline of the Mississippi River are preserved in a natural condition in this park. A useful visitor center provides information regarding the area, while walking trails can be followed down to the river.

Camping: None.

Picnic Area: None.

Water Recreation: Scenic views of the Mississippi River can be enjoyed from the park.

Trails: Hikers and bikers will enjoy the short paved trails that lead to Chase Island. The trails are connected to the Mississippi River Regional Trail, which is a paved path that runs along the river from Anoka in the north to the Anoka County Riverfront Regional Park in the south and connects to the Minneapolis Park System trails.

Recreational Facilities: None.

Seasons: The park is open year-round.

Directions: From Anoka, take County Road 1 south for 8 miles, then follow the park signs.

7. Kordiack County Park

This 29-acre park preserves natural open space around Highland Lake in one of the most densely populated areas of the state. The waterfall and flower garden are highlights of this park.

Camping: None.

Picnic Area: The picnic area features one pavilion, several picnic tables, and restrooms.

Water Recreation: Highland Lake attracts a variety of waterfowl species for viewing.

Trails: A short, paved hiking/biking trail winds around the lake.

Recreational Facilities: A tennis court and playground equipment are provided.

Seasons: The park is open year-round.

Directions: From Anoka, take State Highway 47 south for 10 miles, turn left and take County Road 6 east for 1.5 miles; the park entrance is on the right.

8. Lake George Regional Park

A large, sandy swimming beach makes this park a popular area during the warm summer months. In addition, there are numerous picnic-shelter facilities that can be reserved for large group gatherings.

Camping: None.

Picnic Area: Facilities include seven picnic shelters, several picnic tables, grills, and handicap-accessible restrooms.

Water Recreation: Swimming, boating, and fishing can be enjoyed on Lake George. Facilities include a beach and a concrete boat ramp.

Trails: There are two miles of paved biking/hiking trails provided.

Recreational Facilities: A large creative play structure and sand volleyball courts are provided.

Seasons: The park is open year-round for lake access.

Directions: From Anoka, take County Road 9 north for 12 miles. A vehicle permit is required in the park.

9. Locke County Park

Located in Fridley, Locke County Park's main landscape features include Rice Creek and a thick forest of hardwood trees. A picnic area and a network of trails are also provided.

Camping: None.

Picnic Area: The picnic area features two pavilions, several tables and grills, water, and handicap-accessible restrooms.

Water Recreation: None.

Trails: Several paved hiking/biking trails follow the creek. The Rice Creek West Regional Trail also runs through the park.

Recreational Facilities: A modern play structure is provided.

Seasons: The park is open year-round.

Directions: From Anoka, take State Highway 47 south for 8 miles, then follow the park signs from Highway 47.

10. Manomin County Park

Manomin County Park is located on the Mississippi River and features the Banfill-Locke Tavern, an 1847 building listed on the National Register of Historic Buildings. The building is also home to the Banfill-Locke Center for the Arts.

Camping: None.

Picnic Area: One shelter and several picnic tables are provided within the park.

Restrooms are located next to the south parking lot.

Water Recreation: Riverbank fishing and canoe access is provided.

Trails: A short, paved trail connects the north and south parking lots with the picnic areas, while a gravel trail leads to a viewing deck on the Mississippi River.

Recreational Facilities: None.

Seasons: The park is open year-round.

Directions: From Anoka, take County Road 1 south for 7 miles; watch for the park signs.

11. Martin-Island-Linwood Lakes Regional Park

Over 700 acres of forests, wetlands, and lakes are preserved in their natural condition in this park. Nature study and enjoyment, trails, and lake access are common visitor activities. Large groups can use the rustic group camp for retreats and gatherings.

Camping: The group camp features five cabins, a dining hall, and a restroom/shower building. It can be rented for large groups by contacting the Anoka County Parks and Recreation Department.

Picnic Area: The picnic area features a small shelter, tables, water, and restrooms.

Water Recreation: A small swimming beach is provided on Island Lake. Boat ramps for boating and fishing access are provided on Linwood and Martin lakes.

Trails: Hikers can enjoy 2 miles of trails.

Recreational Facilities: Playground equipment is provided near the beach.

Seasons: The park is open year-round.

Directions: From Anoka, take State Highway 242 east for 5 miles, turn left and go north on County Road 17 for 11 miles, then turn right and go northeast on County Road 22 for 3 miles; follow the park signs from County Road 22. A vehicle permit is required in the park.

12. Rice Creek Chain of Lakes Regional Park Reserve

This park preserves a chain of seven lakes and over 3,000 acres of forest and wetlands. It is unique in that it preserves a large amount of natural habitat in a rapidly developing part of the Twin Cities urban area. It also supports a large blue heron rookery on Peltier Lake.

Camping: The campground features 38 RV sites with water and electrical hookups, 40 rustic tent/RV sites, handicap-accessible restrooms with showers, and an RV dump station. A fee is charged for overnight camping.

Picnic Area: The picnic area on Centerville Lake features a pavilion, picnic tables, and grills.

Water Recreation: A swimming beach with restrooms is located on Centerville Lake. Boat ramps provide fishing and boating access to Peltier and Centerville Lakes. A fishing pier is located on Peltier Lake. A canoe launch on George Watch Lake provides access to the Chain of Lakes Canoe Trail for paddling and portaging on the lakes in the park.

Trails: Visitors can enjoy 4 miles of paved biking/hiking trails, hiking trails near the nature center, and several miles of ski trails.

Recreational Facilities: Playgrounds are provided near the beach and campgrounds. Additional activities include the Chomonix Golf Course, which features 18 scenic holes of golf; a clubhouse with concessions and ski rental; and the Joseph E. Wargo Nature Center. The nature center offers a variety of naturalist programs and outdoor equipment rental throughout the year.

Seasons: The park is open year-round.

Directions: From Anoka, take State Highway 242 east for 14 miles, then follow the park signs. A vehicle permit is required in the park.

(To read more about the park, see "25 Favorite County Parks" in the first section of this guide.)

13. Rum River Central Regional Park

The scenic Rum River provides a backdrop to the prairie and forest landscape of this park. River access, trails, and two picnic areas offer many opportunities for visitor enjoyment. This is one of three parks located on the Rum in Anoka County.

Camping: None.

Picnic Area: The picnic area features a large shelter with electricity, picnic tables and grills, and restrooms.

Water Recreation: Boating, canoeing, and fishing on the Rum River is possible in the park. Facilities include a small boat/canoe launch, carry-in canoe access, and a fishing pier.

Trails: Visitors can enjoy 3 miles of paved biking/hiking trails, 3 miles of hiking/horseback riding trails, and 1.5 miles of ski trails.

Recreational Facilities: A playground is located near the shelter.

Seasons: The park is open year-round.

Directions: From Anoka, take County Road 7 north for 4 miles. A vehicle permit is required in the park.

14. Rum River North County Park

This park preserves 80 acres of shoreline and vegetation along the Rum River in northern Anoka County. Two unique natural features include an oak woodland restoration near the northern picnic area and a prairie restoration area near the south picnic area.

Camping: None.

Picnic Area: The north picnic area features tables, grills, and a handicap-accessible vault toilet. The south picnic area features a picnic pavilion, picnic tables, grills, a year-round meeting building, and handicap-accessible restrooms. The pavilion and meeting room can be reserved.

Water Recreation: A fishing pier and carry-in canoe access to the Rum River is provided.

Trails: Two miles of paved biking/hiking trails offer short loops along the river.

Recreational Facilities: Modern playground equipment is located next to the meeting room building.

Seasons: The park is open year-round.

Directions: From Anoka, take County Road 9 north for 13 miles, County Road 24 west for a half mile, and County Road 72 north for a quarter mile. *(To read more about the park, see "25 Favorite County Parks" in the first section of this guide.)*

15. Rum River South County Park

Picnicking and outdoor enjoyment are provided at this park, which is located on the north side of the city of Anoka. It also features a short trail and boat-ramp access to the river.

Camping: None.

Picnic Area: Facilities include one pavilion with electricity, picnic tables, grills, and a portable toilet.

Water Recreation: Visitors can boat, canoe, or fish on the Rum River. A fishing pier and concrete boat ramp are provided.

Trails: Two miles of paved biking/hiking trails can be found in the park.

Recreational Facilities: A modern creative play structure is provided.

Seasons: The park is open year-round.

Directions: From Anoka, take State Highway 47 north for 1 mile; the park entrance is on the right side of the road.

UNDEVELOPED PARK: Anoka County had one additional park that was undeveloped at the time of this book's publication. Please call of check the county website for up-to-date information regarding this park.

Mississippi West Regional Park
This 270-acre park contains a large amount of Mississippi River frontage and is the site of an old farm. While it obtained park status in 1996, as of this writing it does not have any developed facilities.

Chisago County

Parks Department
38883 7th Avenue
North Branch, MN 55056
(651) 213-6271 or (651) 674-2345
www.co.chisago.mn.us

16. Checkerboard Park
Located in the central part of Chisago County near the town of North Branch, Checkerboard Park offers a quiet setting for picnicking or outdoor enjoyment. It features a few trails and a sand beach located on a small pond.
Camping: None.
Picnic Area: Facilities include a picnic shelter, several picnic tables, and restrooms.
Water Recreation: A small sandy beach provides swimming access to a small pond during the summer season.
Trails: A short hiking trail winds its way around the ponds.
Recreational Facilities: Older-style playground equipment, a volleyball court, and horseshoe pits are provided.
Seasons: The park is open year-round.
Directions: From Interstate 35 at North Branch, take State Highway 95 east for 4 miles and turn left onto County Road 67; the park entrance is on the left side of the road almost immediately after turning from Highway 95.

17. Dennis Frandsen Park
Located in northern Chisago County, Dennis Frandsen Park is the newest and largest park in the Chisago County Park System. It preserves over 100 acres of shoreline, wetlands, and forest on the northern shore of Rush Lake.
Camping: None.

Picnic Area: Facilities include several picnic tables, grills, and a nice-sized shelter for day use. Portable toilets, including one that is handicap-accessible, are provided for sanitation facilities.

Water Recreation: A fishing pier and natural shoreline provide numerous opportunities for shoreline fishing. No boat access was available at the time of this book's publication

Trails: A couple of short trails lead to scenic overlooks along Rush Lake.

Recreational Facilities: None.

Seasons: The park is open year-round.

Directions: From North Branch, take Interstate 35 north for 12 miles to County Road 1; go west, then north on County Road 1 for 5 miles, turn left and go west on County Road 2 for 1.5 miles; the park entrance is on the left side of the road.

18. Fish Lake County Park

Located only minutes from the busy Interstate 35 corridor, this park, relatively unknown to travelers, is very popular with local residents for summertime use. It features a variety of recreation opportunities and is located on the shore of Fish Lake.

Camping: None.

Picnic Area: A nice-sized picnic area features several tables, grills, two shelters, and restrooms. Reservations are accepted for the picnic shelters.

Water Recreation: Canoe, kayak, or motorboat access to Fish Lake is possible through the use of a concrete boat ramp. A medium-sized beach provides swimming access.

Trails: On the opposite side of County Road 65, the park has a few miles of cross-country ski trails open in the winter.

Recreational Facilities: Older-style playground equipment, ball fields, a volleyball court, and horseshoe pits are provided.

Seasons: The park is open year-round.

Directions: From North Branch, take Interstate 35 north for 4.5 miles to County Road 10, go west on County Road 10 for 1.5 miles; then turn left and go south on County Road 65 for a quarter mile; the park entrance is on the right side of the road. A parking fee is charged during the busy summer season.

19. Ki-Chi-Saga Park

Set on a small knoll overlooking South Center Lake and the nearby city of

Ki-Chi-Saga Park features an historic Swedish family home.

Lindstrom, Ki-Chi-Saga Park offers a variety of developed recreation activities. In addition, the Karl Oskar House, a historic Swedish family home, is preserved in the park as an interpretive site in cooperation with the Lindstrom Historical Society.

Camping: None.

Picnic Area: A small, open, grassy picnic area features picnic tables and two shelters.

Water Recreation: None.

Trails: Two-and-a-half miles of hiking trails wind through the open fields and rolling terrain of the park. The trails are also open for cross-country ski use in the winter.

Recreational Facilities: Three ball fields, four soccer fields, modern playground equipment, a volleyball court, and horseshoe pits are provided.

Seasons: The park is open year-round.

Directions: From Chisago City, take Highway 8 northeast for 2.5 miles to County Road 25 in Lindstrom, go south for 1.5 miles on County Road 25, then turn left on Glader Boulevard and go east 1 mile; the park entrance is on the right side of the road.

Relax beside the Sunshine River at Kost Dam Park.

20. Kost Dam Park

Kost Dam Park features a historic dam located on the Sunrise River. Visitors can enjoy picnicking, fishing, and relaxation at this small park.

Camping: None.

Picnic Area: Facilities include several picnic tables, grills, and vault toilet facilities. A second picnic area with tables and grills is located up the road from the park near the entrance from County Road 15.

Water Recreation: Carry-in canoe or small-boat access and fishing opportunities on the Sunrise River are possible, both above and below the spillway dam.

Trails: None.

Recreational Facilities: Older-style playground swings and a slide are provided.

Seasons: The park is open year-round.

Directions: From Interstate 35 at North Branch, take State Highway 95 east for 6.5 miles, turn right and take County Road 9 south for 1.5 miles, then turn right and take County Road 15 southwest for 1.5 miles; the park entrance is on the left side of the road.

Dakota County

Parks Department
14955 Galaxie Avenue
Apple Valley, MN 55124-8579
(952) 891-7000
www.co.dakota.mn.us/parks

21. Lake Byllesby Regional Park

Lake Byllesby, a reservoir on the Cannon River, provides the central focus for this regional park in southern Dakota County. It features a campground, picnic area, boat launch, and beautiful swimming beach on over 500 acres of young trees, wetlands, and prairie.

Camping: The large campground features 35 RV sites with water and electrical hookups and 22 tent sites. All of the RV sites are located along the lakeshore, along with some of the tent sites. Handicap-accessible restrooms with showers and an RV dump station are provided at the camp store building. Portable toilets are located at various locations within the campground. An overnight fee is charged for camping, and reservations are accepted.

Picnic Area: One picnic area is located adjacent to the swimming beach, while the other is near the boat ramp and the tent campground. Both picnic areas feature tables, grills, and the scenic backdrop of Lake Byllesby. A large, open pavilion is also available for large groups.

Water Recreation: Lake Byllesby provides numerous opportunities for fishing, swimming, canoeing, kayaking, motor boating, sailing, and water skiing. The park contains two public boat accesses, one for motorized and one for nonmotorized boats, and a large, sandy beach featuring a marked swimming area.

Trails: Three miles of hiking trails wind through a mix of young trees, wetlands, and prairies within the park.

Recreational Facilities: A large, modern children's playground is provided near the tent campground.

Seasons: The park is open year-round for day use. The campground is open from early May to mid-October.

Directions: Go 35 miles south of the Twin Cities on Highway 52 to County Road 86 just north of Cannon Falls, go west on County Road 86, then almost immediately turn left on Harry Avenue; the park entrance is 1.5 miles south.

22. Lebanon Hills Regional Park

The flagship park of the Dakota County Park System, Lebanon Hills preserves over 2,000 acres of nature within rolling and forested hills. Here, you don't feel like you are anywhere near the major attractions and events of the Minneapolis and Saint Paul area. Numerous recreation opportunities are provided at any one of six trailheads/access locations.

Camping: Located on the west end of the park, the campground features 58 sites with water/sewer/electrical hookups, 24 sites with electrical hookups, and 11 sites with no hookups. The electric-only and no-hookup sites are secluded, with ample vegetative screening between sites. Handicap-accessible restrooms with showers and an RV dump station are provided. An overnight fee is charged for camping, and reservations are accepted.

Picnic Areas: Lebanon Hills features three picnic areas. They are located at Jensen Lake, Holland Lake, and Schulze Lake. Each area features picnic tables, grills, restrooms, and trail access. Jensen and Holland Lakes also feature handicap-accessible picnic shelters.

Water Recreation: Schulze Lake features a large, sandy swimming beach with restrooms and concessions. Holland Lake has a nice, floating fishing pier, and the small chain of lakes between Schulze and Jensen lakes provides a beautiful, 2-mile-long canoe route.

Trails: Thirteen miles of hiking trails, 4 miles of mountain bike trails, and 10 miles of horse trails are provided. The Diamond T Ranch located adjacent to the park provides horse trail rides. Most of the park trails are open to cross-country skiing during the winter months.

Recreational Facilities: Jensen Lake and the campground each have large modern playgrounds.

Seasons: The park is open year-round. The campground is open from early May to mid-October.

Directions: From Minneapolis, take Cedar Avenue south to Cliff Road (County Road 32) in Eagan, then go east on Cliff Road. The mountain-biking trailhead and park campground are south on Johnny Cake Road, the Diamond T Ranch and Jensen Lake are south on Pilot Knob Road, and Holland Lake is adjacent to Highway 32. To get to the park visitor center and beach, follow the Schulze Lake signs.

(To read more about the park, see "25 Favorite County Parks" in the first section of this guide.)

23. Miesville Ravine Park Reserve

Located in the southeastern part of the county, Miesville Ravine preserves and protects the valleys and forests at the confluence of Trout Brook and the Cannon River. The most remote of Dakota County's parks, this preserve provides a quiet retreat within over 1,600 acres of mixed hardwood forest.

Camping: None.

Picnic Area: A small picnic area is located on the shores of the Cannon River. Picnic tables and handicap-accessible vault toilets are provided. Two handicap-accessible picnic shelters are also available for group gatherings and events.

Water Recreation: The Trout Brook and Cannon River offer numerous fishing opportunities. The Cannon River is also very popular for canoeing and tubing.

Trails: Three miles of hiking trails are located along the Trout Brook and Cannon River.

Recreational Facilities: None.

Seasons: The park is open year-round.

Directions: From the Mississippi River in the Twin Cities, take U.S. Highway 52 south for 22 miles to County Road 50 in Hampton, then take State Highway 50 east for 6.50 miles to U.S. Highway 61; continue east on Highway 61 for 2 miles to County Road 91, turn right and take County Road 91 south for 2 miles (the road then turns to gravel); veer right, following the park signs, and go three miles to 280th Street, then take 280th Street (also a gravel road) east 1.5 miles to the park entrance.

24. Spring Lake Park Reserve

Perched atop bluffs along the mighty Mississippi River, Spring Lake Park Preserve provides scenic recreational opportunities and habitat for a variety of wildlife. Spring Lake protects a majority of its acreage in a natural state while providing a variety of recreational opportunities.

Camping: None.

Picnic Area: A large picnic area is located at the main entry point to the park, Schaar's Bluff. Several picnic tables, grills, handicap-accessible restrooms, and two handicap-accessible picnic shelters are available for use.

Water Recreation: The mighty Mississippi River widens at this point and provides a scenic backdrop with several small islands. Access to the river is not possible due to a 150-foot bluff.

Trails: Four miles of hiking trails wind their way throughout the Schaar's Bluff portion of the park. These trails are also open for cross-country skiing in the winter.

Recreational Facilities: Other opportunities include sand volleyball, a model plane airfield, and a large modern playground. Two other unique features are a community garden for use by local residents and an archery trail that provides challenging, archery-target shooting while hiking. The archery trail is located at the west unit of the park.

Seasons: The park is open year-round.

Directions: From the Twin Cities, go south on U.S. Highway 52 to State Highway 55, take that east for 4 miles to County Road 42 in Hastings; turn left and take County Road 42 north for 1.5 miles; the park entrance and sign are on the left side of the road.

(To read more about the park, see "25 Favorite County Parks" in the first section of this guide.)

25. Thompson County Park

Nestled between the heavy traffic of Highway 52 and the residences and businesses of West Saint Paul, Thompson County Park provides a slice of nature amid the hustle and bustle of the southern Twin Cities area. Over 50 acres contains a lake, trails, a picnic area, and the Thompson Park Center/Dakota Lodge.

Camping: None.

Picnic Area: A medium-sized picnic area sits on the northeast shore of the lake and includes a large open-air picnic shelter. Picnic tables, grills, and portable toilets including one handicap-accessible portable toilet are provided.

Water Recreation: Thompson Lake provides a nice backdrop for picnicking and fishing.

Trails: Two miles of hiking trails wind through the park's forest. A 1-mile-long, multiple-use asphalt trail connects the park's north and south boundaries by circling around Thompson Lake. The trails are also open for cross-country skiing in the winter.

Recreational Facilities: Horseshoe pits and a large modern playground are provided. The centerpiece of the park is the Thompson Park Center. This large facility provides space for adult recreation activities and features the Dakota Lodge, a handicap-accessible, four-season event facility that can accommodate over 150 people. A rental fee is charged and reservations are accepted for the lodge.
Seasons: The park is open year-round.
Directions: From Saint Paul, take U.S. Highway 52 for 1.5 miles to Butler Avenue; go west on Butler Avenue for a quarter mile; the park entrance and sign are on the left side of the street.

Isanti County

Parks and Recreation Department
555 18th Ave. SW
Cambridge, MN 55008
(763) 689-8220
www.co.isanti.mn.us

26. Dalbo Memorial Forest

A 40-acre pine and spruce forest characterizes the landscape of this park in northern Isanti County. A majority of the land has been kept in a natural condition, with the only development being a parking lot and trails.
Camping: None.
Picnic Area: None.
Water Recreation: None.
Trails: A 2-mile-long hiking trail includes three wetland crossings using timber walkways.
Recreational Facilities: None.
Seasons: The park is open year-round.
Directions: From Cambridge, take State Highway 95 west for 8 miles, then take County Road 47 north for 4 miles; watch for a small gravel parking lot on the right side of the road.

27. Springvale Park

Forest and prairie cover this park's 200-acre landscape and provide habitat for a variety of plants and animals. Access to the park is provided by 3 miles of trails.
Camping: None.

Picnic Area: None.

Water Recreation: None.

Trails: A half-mile-long paved hiking trail and 2.50 miles of grass trails provide access to the park's mixed forest and prairie areas. A portable toilet is provided at the parking lot.

Recreational Facilities: None.

Seasons: The park is open year-round.

Directions: From Cambridge, take State Highway 95 west for 5 miles; watch for a small paved parking lot on the right side of the road.

28. Wayside Prairie

This small roadside park offers a quiet place to picnic or enjoy a short walk. The hiking trail winds through a pine forest and across wetlands using two boardwalks.

Camping: None.

Picnic Area: Facilities include a shelter, picnic tables, grills, and a portable toilet.

Water Recreation: None.

Trails: A 2.5-mile-long hiking trail includes two segments of boardwalks across the nearby wetland.

Recreational Facilities: None.

Seasons: The park is open year-round.

Directions: From Cambridge, take State Highway 95 west for 3 miles to County Road 10, turn left and take County Road 10 south for 9 miles; the park is on the right side of the road.

UNDEVELOPED PARKS: *Isanti County had three additional parks being devel-oped at the time of this book's publication. Please call or check the county website for up-to-date information regarding these parks.*

Becklin Homestead Park/Wildlife Management Area

Isanti County and the State of Minnesota jointly own this tract of public land on the Rum River. Long-range plans include 2 miles of trails and handicap-accessible hunting access. The park is currently undeveloped.

Vegsund Family County Park

Acquisition of this park is currently taking place.

Westbriar
This is a small, 10-acre park that is currently undeveloped.

Ramsey County

Parks and Recreation Department
2015 North Van Dyke Street
Maplewood, MN 55109-3796
(651) 748-2500
www.co.ramsey.mn.us/parks

29. Bald Eagle–Otter Lakes Regional Park
This park preserves green space around Bald Eagle and Otter Lakes in White Bear Township. A little over 300 acres of this regional park are designated as a park preserve, featuring the Tamarack Nature Center. The nature center offers year-round naturalist and education programs highlighting the plants and wildlife outside its doors.

Camping: None.

Picnic Area: A large shelter, several picnic tables, and handicap-accessible restrooms are provided.

Water Recreation: A concrete ramp provides boating access to Bald Eagle Lake. A handicap-accessible floating fishing pier offers shoreline fishing opportunities.

Trails: A short walking trail is provided along the lake. The Tamarack Nature Center also features nature trails.

Recreational Facilities: A modern play structure is provided.

Seasons: The park is open year-round.

Directions: From Saint Paul, take Highway 61 north for 7 miles to White Bear Township, then turn left on to 120th Street North and watch for the park signs.

30. Battle Creek Regional Park
Relatively undeveloped, this park preserves the natural landscape along the Mississippi River in Saint Paul. There are two sections to the park, separated by a housing development. A biking and hiking trail connects the two.

Camping: None.

Picnic Area: None.

Water Recreation: None.

Trails: Bikers, hikers, and skiers will enjoy several miles of paved trails within the park.

Recreational Facilities: A pet exercise area is also provided.

Seasons: The park is open year-round.

Directions: In Saint Paul, take Highway 61 south to Lower Afton Road and watch for the park signs.

31. Beaver Lake County Park

This is a day-use park that surrounds Beaver Lake on the east side of Saint Paul. Visitors can enjoy a picnic, shoreline fishing, or lakeside relaxation.

Camping: None.

Picnic Area: Facilities include a small shelter, picnic tables, grills, and restrooms.

Water Recreation: A handicap-accessible fishing pier provides fishing access to the lake.

Trails: None.

Recreational Facilities: Additional facilities include playground equipment.

Seasons: The park is open from May through September.

Directions: From Saint Paul, take County Road 65 to Stillwater Boulevard, go east for 1 mile, then follow the signs.

32. Island Lake County Park

A grassy, open landscape with several trees welcomes visitors to this park. It features a large picnic area with several shelters and fishing access to Island Lake.

Camping: None.

Picnic Area: Facilities include three shelters, picnic tables, grills, and handicap-accessible restrooms.

Water Recreation: Access to the small lake is provided by a fishing pier and boat ramp.

Trails: A few biking/hiking trails connect the picnic area to a nature area.

Recreational Facilities: A large modern play structure is provided in the picnic area. The Island Golf Course featuring nine holes is located on the west side of the park.

Seasons: The park is open from May through September.

Directions: From Saint Paul, take County Road 52 north for 8 miles.

33. Keller Regional Park

This park's landscape includes three lakes and offers scenic picnicking, walking, and lake access opportunities. It also features a championship golf course.

Camping: None.

Picnic Area: Facilities include one picnic area on Spoon Lake, three picnic areas on Keller Lake, one picnic area between Keller and Round lakes, and one picnic area on Round Lake. All the areas include picnic tables and grills.

Water Recreation: A ramp provides boating and fishing access to Spoon Lake, while a handicap-accessible fishing pier offers shoreline fishing opportunities on Round Lake.

Trails: Some short trails are provided.

Recreational Facilities: The 18-hole Keller Golf Course occupies the eastern portion of this park.

Seasons: The park is open spring through fall.

Directions: The park is located along U.S. Highway 61 between State Highway 36 and County Road 26 in Maplewood.

34. Lake Gervais County Park

This is a small day-use area located in the southwestern corner of Lake Gervais. It features a swimming beach and a picnic area.

Camping: None.

Picnic Area: A small shelter, picnic tables, and grills are provided.

Water Recreation: A sandy beach provides swimming access to the lake. A restroom/bathhouse building is located next to the beach.

Trails: None.

Recreational Facilities: Additional facilities include playground equipment.

Seasons: The park is open from May through September.

Directions: In Little Canada, take State Highway 36 to Edgerton Street, turn north and go a half mile to the park.

35. Lake Josephine County Park

Lake Josephine provides a scenic backdrop to this developed park located in Roseville. It features picnicking, swimming, and lake access opportunities.

Camping: None.

Picnic Area: Facilities include picnic tables and restrooms.

Water Recreation: Access to the lake is provided by a swimming beach and a boat ramp.

Trails: None.

Recreational Facilities: A modern play structure is provided.

Seasons: The park is open from spring through fall.

Directions: From Saint Paul, take County Road 51 (Lexington Avenue) north for 5 miles to the park on the east shore of Lake Josephine.

36. Lake McCarrons County Park

This park contains a nice mixture of trees and grass set on Lake McCarrons. It features picnicking, swimming, and lake access opportunities.

Camping: None.

Picnic Area: Facilities include one medium-sized shelter, picnic tables, grills, and a restroom/bathhouse building.

Water Recreation: A swimming beach, fishing pier, and boat ramp provide access to the lake.

Trails: A few biking/hiking trails run through the park's landscape.

Recreational Facilities: Playground equipment is provided.

Seasons: The park is open from May through September.

Directions: In Roseville, take Rice Street (County Road 49) to Center Street, turn west and go a short distance.

37. Lake Owasso County Park

Picnicking, swimming, and lake access is provided in this park located between Lake Owasso and Lake Wabasso. There are enough shelters and tables to accommodate several large groups.

Camping: None.

Picnic Area: Facilities include three medium-sized shelters, picnic tables, grills, and a restroom/bathhouse building.

Water Recreation: A swimming beach on Lake Owasso and boat ramps on both lakes are provided.

Trails: None.

Recreational Facilities: Playground equipment is provided.

Seasons: The park is open from May through September.

Directions: From Saint Paul, take County Road 49 north for 4 miles, turn left and go west on Lake Owasso Boulevard North (County Road 18) for a half mile.

38. Long Lake Regional Park

Picnicking, trails, and water-related activities can be enjoyed in this park, which is located in the city of New Brighton. Visitors can explore a historic walking tour in the park that describes the area during the late 1800s and early 1900s. It was developed by the New Brighton Area Historical Society, whose history center is located along the park entrance road.

Camping: None.

Picnic Area: Facilities include an extra-large shelter, a small shelter, picnic tables, and grills.

Water Recreation: A concrete ramp provides boating and fishing access to Long Lake, while swimmers will enjoy the large, sandy swimming beach. A concessions building with handicap-accessible restrooms is located near the beach.

Trails: Paved biking, hiking, and skiing trails are provided.

Recreational Facilities: Three modern play structures are provided near the shelters and the beach.

Seasons: The park is open year-round.

Directions: From Saint Paul, take Interstate 35W north for 5 miles to State Highway 96, turn west and follow the park signs.

39. Tony Schmidt County Park

This good-sized park preserves a landscape of hardwood trees within residential developments. It features a variety of land- and water-based recreational activities.

Camping: None.

Picnic Area: Facilities include two shelters, picnic tables, grills, and handicap-accessible restrooms.

Water Recreation: Boating, fishing, and swimming access to Lake Johanna is provided by a boat ramp and a beach. A restroom/changing house building is also provided.

Trails: None.

Recreational Facilities: Three playgrounds and a ball field are provided.

Seasons: The park is open from spring through fall.

Directions: From Saint Paul, take Snelling Avenue (State Highway 51) north for 7 miles, then turn left and take Lake Johanna Boulevard west for 1 mile.

40. Turtle Lake County Park

Large oak and elm trees shade the landscape of this small park. It features a swimming beach, relaxing picnic area, and boat access on only a few acres.

Camping: None.

Picnic Area: Two small shelters, picnic tables, and restrooms are provided.
Water Recreation: A concrete ramp provides access to Turtle Lake. A small swimming beach is supervised by lifeguards during the summer season.
Trails: None.
Recreational Facilities: Playground equipment and a baseball/softball field is provided.
Seasons: The park is open from early May through late September.
Directions: From Saint Paul, take Interstate 35E north for 10 miles to Interstate 694, turn west onto I-694 and go one mile to County Road 49; take it north for 8 miles to the park, which is on the left side of the road.

41. Vadnais–Snail Lakes Regional Park

This park preserves several acres of natural forest and wetlands within the

Swimmers flock to Vadnais-Snail Lakes Regional Park.

confines of urban Ramsey County. Visitors can enjoy trails, picnic areas, and a swimming beach.

Camping: None.

Picnic Area: Two picnic areas offer several opportunities to enjoy a meal outdoors. One extra-large shelter and one medium-sized shelter can be re-served for large gatherings. Numerous picnic tables and a handicap-accessible restroom/bathhouse are also provided.

Water Recreation: Double concrete ramps and a handicap-accessible fishing pier provide boating and fishing access to Snail Lake. Swimmers can enjoy a large beach that is supervised by lifeguards during the summer season.

Trails: Several miles of biking, hiking, snowshoeing, and skiing trails wind their way through the forested landscape of this regional park.

Recreational Facilities: Volleyball courts and a modern play structure are provided.

Seasons: The park is open year-round.

Directions: From Saint Paul, take Interstate 35E north for 10 miles to Interstate 694, turn west onto I-694 and go 1 mile to County Road 49; take that north for 4 miles, then turn left and follow the signs to the park's main picnic areas.

42. White Bear Lake County Park

Located on the west shore of White Bear Lake, this park is a popular swimming and picnicking destination. On any nice summer day it will be crowded with kids and adults escaping the heat with a swim in the lake.

Camping: None.

Picnic Area: Numerous picnic tables and grills are spread out along the beachfront area. A handicap-accessible restroom/bathhouse building is also provided.

Water Recreation: A concrete ramp provides access to White Bear Lake. The main attraction to this park is the large, sandy swimming beach that is staffed by lifeguards during the summer.

Trails: A short, paved trail winds through the park.

Recreational Facilities: A large, modern play structure is provided.

Seasons: The beach is open and staffed by lifeguards from approximately mid-June until mid-August. The public water access is open year-round.

Directions: From Saint Paul, take U.S. Highway 61 north for 6 miles, then turn right and go a half mile east on State Highway 96; the park is on the right side of the road.

Sherburne County

Parks and Recreation Department
13880 Highway 10
Elk River, MN 55330-4601
(763) 241-2939
www.co.sherburne.mn.us

43. Bridgeview Park Reserve

Native hardwood forest, grasses, and Mississippi River shoreline are protected within this park. A majority of the park has been kept in its natural condition, and a network of trails is designed to allow visitors to explore and enjoy the landscape.

Camping: None.

Picnic Area: None.

Water Recreation: None.

Trails: Short walking trails are provided and mowed for year-round hiking and snowshoeing use.

Recreational Facilities: None.

Seasons: The park is open year-round.

Directions: From Elk River, take U.S. Highway 10 northwest for 12 miles, then take County Road 50 south for 2 miles.

44. Grams Regional Park

With over 100 acres of land and 1,000 feet of shoreline on Fremont Lake, this park offers a varied landscape of rolling hills, wetlands, grassy areas, and oak forest. In the early development stages at the time of this book's publication, it features some hiking trails and scenic vistas.

Camping: None.

Picnic Area: None.

Water Recreation: Although located on Fremont Lake, the park has no designated lake access at the time of this book's publication.

Trails: Short hiking trails are provided.

Recreational Facilities: None.

Seasons: The park is open year-round.

Directions: From Elk River, take U.S. Highway 169 north for 7 miles, take County Road 4 east for three-quarters of a mile, then take 120th Street north for 1 mile.

45. Oak Savanna Land Preserve

As the name indicates, this park features an oak landscape and also includes pine forests and prairie grasses. A majority of the park remains in a natural condition with trails as the only development.

Camping: None.

Picnic Area: None.

Water Recreation: None.

Trails: A series of trails are provided for hiking, mountain biking, horseback riding, snowshoeing, skiing, and dogsledding. The trails connect with Becker City Park to offer additional trail mileage.

Recreational Facilities: None.

Seasons: The park is open year-round.

Directions: From Elk River, take Highway 10 northwest for 16.5 miles, then take County Road 23 north for 1 mile; watch for the Becker City Park sign (current access is through Becker City Park).

Washington County

County Parks Division
1515 Keats Avenue North
Lake Elmo, MN 55042
(651) 430-8368
www.co.washington.mn.us/parks

46. Big Marine Park Reserve

Located on Big Marine Lake, this is the newest addition to Washington County Parks. At the time of this book's printing it was in the early stages of development. Its landscape will include upland and wetland habitats in addition to lakeshore.

Camping: None.

Picnic Area: None.

Water Recreation: A concrete boat ramp provides access to Big Marine Lake. A portable toilet is provided.

Trails: None.

Recreational Facilities: None.

Seasons: The park is open from April through October.

Directions: From Stillwater, take County Road 12 west for 2 miles, take

County Road 15 north for 9 miles to Lomond Road, then turn right and go east for 1 mile. A vehicle permit is required in the park.

47. Cottage Grove Ravine Regional Park

Cottage Grove Ravine Regional Park is located in southern Washington County on the northern edge of the Mississippi River valley. It preserves nearly 500 acres of rolling hills and ravines that are covered by a mixed hardwood forest and scattered pine trees.

Camping: None.

Picnic Area: Facilities include several picnic tables, cooking grills, and a moderate-sized, handicap-accessible picnic shelter. Reservations are recommended and a fee is charged for shelter use. Handicap-accessible restrooms are also provided in the shelter.

Water Recreation: A pond provides a scenic view of water and wildlife habitat, but it isn't large enough for water-recreation use.

Cottage Grove Ravine Regional Park offers modern facilities and 500 acres of rolling hills and ravines.

Trails: The park offers 7 miles of hiking/walking trails that wind through the mixed hardwood forest. A paved bicycle trail runs from the southern end of the park to its northern boundary and a nearby county road. During the winter, approximately 7 miles of cross-country ski trails are groomed for visitor use.

Recreational Facilities: A modern playground structure is located in the center of the picnic area.

Seasons: The park is open year-round.

Directions: From the junction of Interstate 494 and U.S. Highway 61/10 (north of Saint Paul Park), go approximately 9 miles southeast on Highway 61/10 to the County Road 19 exit; go north to the frontage road and turn right on it; the park entrance is on the left side of the road (follow the signs). A vehicle permit is required in the park.

48. Lake Elmo Park Reserve

Lake Elmo Park Reserve is the largest park in Washington County's system. As a park reserve, only 20 percent of its acreage can be developed, while the other 80 percent must remain in its natural state. It features numerous recreational opportunities within easy driving distance of the eastern Twin Cities metropolitan area.

Camping: Facilities include a large, modern campground with 80 sites, and each is equipped with electrical hookups, a picnic table, and a fire ring. Handicap-accessible restrooms with showers, water, and an RV dump station are also provided. A 20-site campground is provided near the equestrian trails. Facilities include a hand pump for water and portable toilets for sanitation. Three group camping areas can accommodate up to 100 campers each in primitive camping and natural settings. Portable toilets are provided, and the restrooms/showers of the regular campground are within walking distance. Fees are charged for all types of overnight camping.

Picnic Areas: Several picnic areas are located throughout the park. Numerous picnic tables and grills are provided. In addition, two large, handicap-accessible picnic shelters, with electricity, water, restrooms, picnic tables, and adequate parking, are available for rental use. Shelters can be reserved in advance and a fee is charged for their use.

Water Recreation: The park features access to Lake Elmo and Eagle Point Lake. A canoe access is provided to Eagle Point Lake. A fishing pier and boat ramp provides access to Lake Elmo. Swimming opportunities are provided at a unique swimming pond that is filtered and disinfected. The pond is only six feet deep and features a gently sloping, sandy bottom. A nice, sandy beach surrounds the pond and includes grassy picnic areas, handicap-accessible restrooms, a changing house, and a concession stand.

Trails: The park offers numerous land-recreation opportunities on over 2,000 acres of rolling hills, prairies, and forested areas. Twenty miles of hiking trails wind throughout the park. Eight miles of the trails are open for horseback riding and mountain-bike riding. Twelve miles of trails are groomed for cross-country skiing in the winter.

Recreational Facilities: A large, modern playground, softball field, volleyball court, and horseshoe pits are provided. Another unique facility provided is a multitarget archery range.

Seasons: The park is open year-round. The camping facilities are open from early May to mid-October. The swimming facility is open from Memorial Day to Labor Day.

Directions: From Stillwater, take State Highway 5 south for 5 miles to County Road 17 at Lake Elmo, take CR 17 for 2.5 miles to County Road 10, turn right on County Road 10, and go west for 1 mile; the park entrance is located on the right side of the road. A vehicle permit is required in the park.

49. Pine Point Park

Once the site of a county-owned farm, Pine Point Park now offers dispersed recreation opportunities. Hiking, cross-country skiing, and horseback-riding trails are provided for visitor use.

Camping: None.

Picnic Area: A few picnic tables and handicap-accessible restrooms are located at the trailhead parking lot.

Water Recreation: None.

Trails: Pine Point offers access to the paved Gateway Trail segment of the Willard-Munger State Trail. It also features 5 miles of trails for hiking, skiing, and horseback riding. The trails are groomed for cross-country skiing during the winter.

Recreational Facilities: None.

Seasons: The park is open year-round.

Directions: From Stillwater, take County Road 55 north for 4 miles; the park entrance is located on the left side of the road, near the junction with County Road 61. A vehicle permit is required in the park.

50. Point Douglas Park

Situated on the north side of the peninsula of land where the Mississippi and Saint Croix Rivers converge, Point Douglas Park offers scenic picnicking and nice swimming opportunities for residents and visitors. It also offers a convenient wayside rest for visitors traveling along U.S. Highway 10, the Great River Road.

Camping: None.

Picnic Area: Facilities include a picnic area with tables and grills spread along the river's shoreline. Restrooms are available during the summer, and a portable toilet is provided during the winter.

Water Recreation: A nice, sandy beach provides swimming access to the waters of the Saint Croix River. A handicap-accessible restroom/changing house is provided.

Trails: A short walking trail leads to a viewing platform on the river near the Prescott drawbridge.

Recreational Facilities: None.

Seasons: The park is open year-round. The beach is open from Memorial Day to Labor Day.

Directions: From the junction of Interstate 494 and U.S. Highway 61/10 (north of Saint Paul Park), go approximately 14 miles southeast on Highway 61/10, then turn left and go east for 3 miles on U.S. Highway 10; the park is on the left side of the road just before Prescott, Wisconsin.

51. Saint Croix Bluffs Regional Park

Saint Croix Bluffs Regional Park is located on the scenic Saint Croix River (a National Wild and Scenic River) in southeastern Washington County. It offers numerous camping and recreational opportunities while preserving nearly 4,000 feet of natural shoreline and acres of natural hardwood forest, which provide habitat for a variety of wildlife.

Camping: A large campground features 21 RV sites with water and electricity, 41 RV sites with electricity, and 11 sites with no hookups. Each site is provided with a table and a fire ring, and the campground also contains a handicap-accessible restroom/shower building. An RV dump station is also provided. A fee is charged for overnight camping.

Picnic Area: Facilities include three handicap-accessible shelters and numerous picnic tables and grills. The shelters (with names like Birch Hollow and Eagle Ridge) can be reserved, and a rental fee is charged for their use. Water, electricity, and a nearby restroom are provided.

Water Recreation: The park offers a double concrete boat ramp and a large parking lot providing access to the waters of the Saint Croix River.

Trails: Five miles of hiking trails are provided. During the winter the trails are groomed for cross-country skiing.

Recreational Facilities: Modern playgrounds are provided in the campground and in the picnic area. The picnic area also features tennis courts, horseshoe pits, a volleyball court, and an open softball field.

Seasons: The park is open year-round. The campground is open from early May through mid-October.

Directions: From the junction of Interstate 494 and U.S. Highway 61/10 (north of Saint Paul Park), go approximately 14 miles southeast on Highway 61/10, then turn left and go east on Highway 10 for 2 miles; turn left on County Road 21 and go north for 4 miles; the park entrance is on the right side of the road. A vehicle permit is required in the park.

(To read more about the park, see "25 Favorite County Parks" in the first section of this guide.)

52. Square Lake County Park

Square Lake County Park is located north of Stillwater and features a large, sandy beach and boat access. Visitors can enjoy swimming, picnicking, and boating opportunities within this small park.

Camping: None.

Picnic Area: Facilities include numerous picnic tables and grills. A handicap-accessible changing house with restrooms and a concession stand are also provided.

Water Recreation: The central focus of this park is a very large and sandy swimming beach that can accommodate large numbers of visitors on hot summer days. A floating fishing pier and concrete boat ramp also provide fishing and boat/canoe access to Square Lake.

Trails: None.

Recreational Facilities: None.

Seasons: The park is open year-round. The swimming beach and building facilities are open from Memorial Day to Labor Day.

Directions: From Stillwater, take County Road 55 north for 5. miles, then turn right on County Road 7 and go east for 3 miles; the park entrance is located on the left side of the road. A vehicle permit is required in the park.

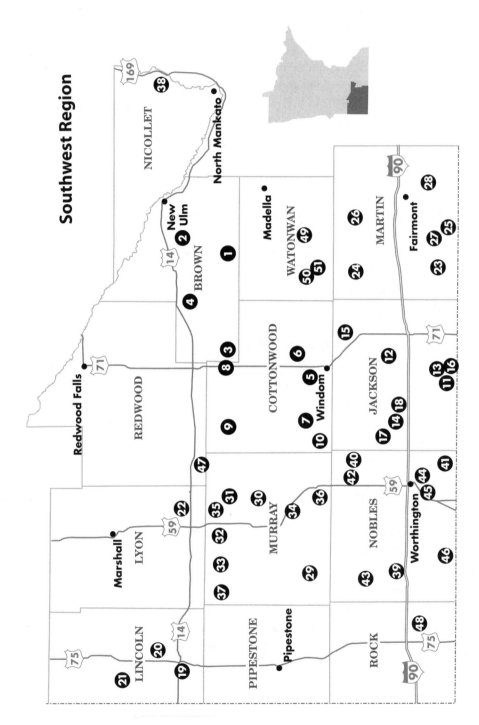

Southwest Region

NICOLLET

169

38

North Mankato

New Ulm

14

2

BROWN

4

1

Madelia

WATONWAN

49

50 51

MARTIN

90

28

26

27 25

24

23

Fairmont

COTTONWOOD

3

8

6

15

5

Windom

7

9

10

JACKSON

12

13 16

11

14 18

17

71

REDWOOD

Redwood Falls

71

47

MURRAY

31

35

30

34

36

32

33

37

29

42 40

59

NOBLES

43

39

46

Worthington

45 44

41

LYON

59

Marshall

22

LINCOLN

75

20

21

14

19

PIPESTONE

Pipestone

ROCK

48

75

90

SOUTHWEST REGION

Brown County

Park Department
PO Box 248, Courthouse
New Ulm, MN 56073
(507) 233-6640
www.co.brown.mn.us

1. Lake Hanska County Park

Lake Hanska County Park features 140 acres of historical features and recreational opportunities. It is located on the largest lake in Brown County. Visitors can enjoy camping, swimming, picnicking, hiking, or boating at this park.

Camping: The campground includes several RV sites with electricity, wooded tent sites, handicap-accessible restrooms with showers, and an RV dump station. A fee is charged for overnight camping.

Picnic Area: Facilities include three shelters, picnic tables, grills, and a water pump.

Water Recreation: Lake Hanska offers boating, swimming, and fishing opportunities. The park features a sandy swimming beach and fishing dock. A public boat ramp is located nearby.

Trails: Several miles of hiking and skiing trails are provided.

Recreational Facilities: Playground equipment is provided.

Seasons: The park is open from May through September.

Directions: From New Ulm, take U.S. Highway 14 west for 5 miles, then turn left and go south on County Road 11 for 14 miles.

2. Lost Dog and Fox Hunter's County Park

Named after the club that donated the land for the park, this is one of the more colorfully named county parks in Minnesota. It features a nice, shaded picnic area and lake access.

Camping: None.

Picnic Area: Facilities include two shelters with electricity, picnic tables, grills, a water pump, and vault toilets.

Water Recreation: Clear Lake offers fishing and boating opportunities. Shoreline and dock fishing is possible in the park. A boat ramp is also located nearby.

Trails: None.

Recreational Facilities: Playground equipment and a volleyball court are provided.

Seasons: The park is open from May through September.

Directions: From New Ulm, take County Road 13 south for 2 miles, turn right and go west on County Road 25 for 1 mile, then follow the signs from County Road 25.

3. Mound Creek County Park

Three hundred acres of rolling hills, prairie, and a 70-acre reservoir lake highlight the landscape of this park, which is located in the southwestern corner of Brown County. The most unique feature is seeing the open waterfalls that flow over bedrock outcroppings during high water periods. The waterfall is only a short hike from the parking lot.

Camping: None.

Picnic Area: Two shelters, picnic tables, grills, and vault toilets are provided.

Water Recreation: A concrete boat ramp provides boating and fishing access to the reservoir, while a small, sandy beach provides swimming access to the same waters.

Trails: Three miles of hiking trails are provided.

Recreational Facilities: Open play fields, sand volleyball, and a nine-hole disc golf course are provided.

Seasons: The park is open from April 15 to October 15.

Directions: From New Ulm, take U.S. Highway 14 west for 36 miles to the junction with U.S. Highway 71, turn left and go south on Highway 71 for 9 miles, turn left and go east on County Road 10 for 2 miles, then turn left and go north on 450th Ave.

(To read more about the park, see "25 Favorite County Parks" in the first section of this guide.)

4. Treml County Park

As the site of a former farmstead, this park features a little bit of local history and a nice, shady setting on Altermatt Lake. Visitors can enjoy picnicking and fishing from shore.

Camping: None.

Picnic Area: A shelter with electricity, picnic tables, grills, and vault toilets are provided.

Water Recreation: Shoreline fishing on Altermatt Lake is possible in the park.

Trails: A few short hiking trails wind through the park.

Recreational Facilities: None.

Seasons: The park is open from May through September.

Directions: From New Ulm, take U.S. Highway 14 west for 14 miles to State Highway 4 in Sleepy Eye, turn left and go south on for 7 miles; turn right and go west on County Road 22 for 4 miles, then follow County Road 100 for 2 miles.

Cottonwood County

Parks Department
235 9th Street
Windom, MN 56101
(507) 831-2060
www.rronet.org/~cotton/cotpeak.html

5. Dynamite Park

Located within the city of Windom, this small park was once the storage site for the county highway department's dynamite and other equipment.

Camping: None.

Picnic Area: Facilities include a shelter house with a fireplace and tables.

Water Recreation: None.

Trails: None.

Recreational Facilities: A basketball court and playground are provided.

Seasons: The shelter house can be used year-round.

Directions: In Windom, take River Road north a short distance; the park is on the left side of the road adjacent to the golf course.

6. Mountain County Park

This park features a raised island of land that stands above the nearby fields that were once the bottom of a lake. The island landscape has been left in its natural state for wildlife and bird habitat.

Camping: None.

Picnic Area: An old shelter, playground equipment, and vault toilets are not maintained and are currently unusable.

Water Recreation: None.

Trails: None.

Recreational Facilities: None.

Seasons: The park is open year-round.

Directions: From Windom, take State Highway 60 northeast for 12 miles, then turn right and go south on 600th Avenue for 1.5 miles; the park entrance is on the right side of the road.

7. Pat's Grove

This 80-acre park is located at the confluence of the Des Moines River and the Heron Lake outlet. It features a historic 1878 stone house and a mixed forest of basswood, oak, and black walnut trees.

Camping: None.

Picnic Area: A few picnic tables and fire rings are provided.

Water Recreation: The Des Moines River flows through the park.

Trails: None.

Recreational Facilities: None.

Seasons: The park is open from April through October.

Directions: From Windom, take State Highway 62 west for 9 miles to 390th Avenue, turn right and go north for 1 mile; the park entrance is on the right side of the road.

8. Red Rock Falls Park

Red Rock Falls Park is perhaps the most unique, undiscovered county park in the state. It features a small hollow with exposed, red-colored bedrock 30 feet deep, with a stream and waterfall running through the hollow.

Camping: None.

Picnic Area: An old shelter, playground equipment, and vault toilets are not maintained and are currently unusable. The grass is still mowed so it is possible to walk around the picnic area.

Water Recreation: Hidden among the trees just behind the picnic area are the Red Rock Mini-Dells with Mound Creek running into them. Please be careful and keep children close at hand near the edges, as it is a 30-foot drop to the bottom.

Trails: A short trail from the picnic area leads to Red Rock Falls.

Recreational Facilities: None.

Seasons: The park is open year-round.

Directions: From Windom, take U.S. Highway 71 north for 17 miles, then turn right and go east on 250th Street for a half mile.

(To read more about the park, see "25 Favorite County Parks" in the first section of this guide.)

9. South Dutch Charlie Park

This park is named after Cottonwood County's first European settler. It is located along the Dutch Charlie Creek in a small valley.

Camping: Facilities include four campsites with electricity, tables, fire rings, and vault toilets. No fee is charged for camping.

Picnic Area: A shelter, picnic tables, and grills are provided.

Water Recreation: None.

Trails: None.

Recreational Facilities: None.

Seasons: The park is open from April through October.

Directions: From Windom, take State Highway 62 west for 13 miles to County Road 6, turn right and go north for 15 miles; the park entrance is on the left side of the road.

10. Talcot Lake County Park

This is a popular campground located on Talcot Lake in the far-western section of the county. It features several RV and tent campsites, a swimming beach, a picnic area, and boat access to the lake.

Camping: The large campground features 54 RV sites with electricity, water, tables, fire rings, modern restrooms with showers, vault toilets, and an RV dump station. A tenting area is located near the beach. Campground staff members are on duty at the office, and fees are charged for overnight camping.

Picnic Area: Facilities include a shelter house, picnic tables, and grills near the beach and picnic tables and grills near the public boat access.

Water Recreation: Boating, fishing, and swimming opportunities are provided, including a concrete boat ramp, a fishing pier, and beach facilities on Talcot Lake.

Trails: None.

Recreational Facilities: Playground equipment is provided near the beach.

Seasons: The park is open from April through October.

Directions: From Windom, take State Highway 62 west for 16 miles; the park entrance is on the right side of the road.

Jackson County

Parks Department
405 4th Street
Jackson, MN 56143
(507) 847-2240
www.co.jackson.mn.us

11. Anderson County Park

With a large campground and access to Pearl Lake, this park is popular with local residents and visitors. In addition to the campground, it offers a nice picnic area. Along with nearby Brown Park and Robertson Park, Anderson forms a nice trio of county parks to choose from.

Camping: The campground features 25 RV/tent sites with electricity, tables, fire rings, an RV dump station, and modern restrooms with showers. A fee is charged for overnight camping.

Picnic Area: Facilities include one shelter with a fireplace and electricity, picnic tables, grills, and water.

Water Recreation: A boat ramp provides boating and fishing access to Pearl Lake.

Trails: None.

Recreational Facilities: A Frisbee-disc golf course and observation tower are provided.

Seasons: The park is open from May through September.

Directions: From Jackson, take Interstate 90 west for 9 miles to State Highway 86, turn left and go south for 7.5 miles, turn left and go east on County Road 4 for 2.5 miles.

12. Belmont County Park

Nature study opportunities can be enjoyed at this park, which is located on the Des Moines River. It features a picnic area, trails, and river access.

Camping: None.

Picnic Area: Facilities include a shelter with electricity, picnic tables, grills, water, and vault toilets.

Water Recreation: Canoeing or fishing are available on the Des Moines River.
Trails: A short, self-guided nature trail allows visitors the opportunity to enjoy the trees and plants of the park.
Recreational Facilities: None.
Seasons: The park is open year-round.
Directions: From Jackson, take U.S. Highway 71 north for 6.5 miles, then turn left and go west on County Road 76 for 2 miles.

13. Brown County Park

Large oak trees tower over the picnic area of this park, which is located between Pearl and Loon lakes. It also features a campground and access to both lakes for boating and fishing. Brown Park can be conveniently visited along with nearby Anderson Park and Robertson Park.

Camping: The campground features 30 RV sites with electricity, water, tables, fire rings, and modern restrooms with showers. A small, grassy area is designated for tent camping between the campground and picnic area. Park caretakers live nearby at Robertson County Park and a fee is charged for overnight camping.
Picnic Area: The picnic area includes one large shelter with a fireplace and electricity, picnic tables, grills, water, and vault toilets. A small footbridge over a creek connects the picnic area to the campground.
Water Recreation: Small boats and canoes can be carried in to access Pearl Lake. A boat ramp and fishing pier are located on the Loon Lake side of the park.
Trails: None.
Recreational Facilities: Playground equipment is provided both in the campground and picnic area.
Seasons: The park is open from May through September.
Directions: From Jackson, take Interstate 90 west for 9 miles to State Highway 86, turn left and go south for 7.5 miles, turn left and go east on County Road 4 for 3 miles.

14. Community Point County Park

Picnicking and bird watching can be enjoyed at this small park, which is located on the east side of South Heron Lake. It features a small picnic shelter house and a sandy shoreline. It is one of two county parks on the lake (Sandy Point is the other).

Camping: None.
Picnic Area: A shelter house with electricity and fireplace, picnic tables, grills,

water, and vault toilets are provided.

Water Recreation: A sandy shoreline allows swimming and small-boat access to South Heron Lake. The lake features special regulations during waterfowl migration. Please check with the state DNR for further details.

Trails: None.

Recreational Facilities: Playground equipment is provided.

Seasons: The park is open year-round.

Directions: From Jackson take Interstate 90 west for 9 miles, take State Highway 86 north for 4 miles, then turn left and go west on County Road 71 for 1.5 miles.

15. Obie Knutson County Park

This is a small, day-use park located on the south shore of Fish Lake. It is primarily used for picnicking, lake access, and fishing access.

Camping: None.

Picnic Area: Facilities include a shelter, picnic tables, and vault toilets.

Water Recreation: A nearby boat ramp provides access to Fish Lake.

Trails: None.

Recreational Facilities: Playground equipment is provided.

Seasons: The park is open year-round.

Directions: From Jackson, take Highway 71 north for 15 miles, then turn right and go east on County Road 84 for 1 mile.

16. Robertson County Park

This is a heavily forested park located on the east side of Loon Lake. Cultural surveys of the area have determined that this is one of the more significant archaeological sites in Jackson County. The landscape can be explored by hiking a few miles of trails. Nearby are Anderson Park and Brown Park, all located conveniently within a mile of one another.

Camping: The developed campground features 22 RV sites with electricity, water, tables, fire rings, modern restrooms with showers, and an RV dump station. Additional primitive campsites near the picnic areas allow for more camping during the peak season. A park caretaker lives on-site and operates a camp store. A fee is charged for overnight camping.

Picnic Area: The picnic area includes one large shelter with a fireplace and electricity, picnic tables, grills, water, and vault toilets.

Water Recreation: A boat ramp provides boating and fishing opportunities on Loon Lake.

Trails: Hikers can enjoy a few miles of trails within the park's 46 acres.

Recreational Facilities: Playground equipment is provided both in the campground and picnic area.

Seasons: The park is open from May through September.

Directions: From Jackson, take Interstate 90 west for 9 miles to State Highway 86, turn left and go south for 7.5 miles, turn left and go east on County Road 4 for 3.50 miles.

17. Sandy Point County Park

Located on the west shore of South Heron Lake, this park offers a perfect location for viewing the waterfowl that make Heron Lake their home. The lake is considered one of the best waterfowl-production areas in the state. Sandy Point is one of two county parks on the lake (Community Point Park is located on the east shore).

Camping: The campground features 12 RV sites with electricity, tables, fire rings, and vault toilets. A fee is charged for overnight camping.

Picnic Area: The picnic area includes one large shelter house with a fireplace and electricity, picnic tables, grills, water, and vault toilets.

Water Recreation: A boat ramp and sandy shoreline provide boating and fishing access to South Heron Lake.

Trails: None.

Recreational Facilities: Playground equipment, volleyball courts, and open fields are provided. Wildlife observation is enhanced by an observation tower near the picnic area.

Seasons: The park is open from April through October.

Directions: From Jackson, take Interstate 90 west for 9 miles to State Highway 86, turn right and go north for 3 miles, then turn left and go west on County Road 20 for 3.5 miles; follow the signs from County Road 20.
(To read more about the park, see "25 Favorite County Parks" in the first section of this guide.)

18. Sparks Environmental County Park

Located on the edge of the town of Lakefield, this 40-acre natural area is home to the Prairie Ecology Bus Center. It provides environmental education programs to youth throughout the year.

Camping: None.

Picnic Area: None.

Water Recreation: None.

Trails: None.

Recreational Facilities: None.

Seasons: The Prairie Ecology Bus Center provides programs throughout the year. For more information call (507) 662-5064.

Directions: From Jackson, take Interstate 90 west for 9 miles to State Highway 86, turn right and go north for 3 miles; the park is on the north side of Lakefield.

Lincoln County

County Parks
PO Box 369
Lake Benton, MN 56149
(507) 368-9350
www.co.lincoln.mn.us/Departments/Parks.htm

19. Hole in the Mountain County Park

Hole in the Mountain takes advantage of 800 acres of steep slopes on the Buffalo Ridge for trails and a downhill ski area. Buffalo Ridge is a glacial feature that is famous for being the windiest spot in Minnesota. From the park you can see some of the large wind generators that have been placed on the ridge, which take advantage of the wind to generate electricity from a renewable resource.

> **Camping:** The campground includes 17 RV/tent sites with electricity and water located near the chalet and an additional 12 undeveloped campsites for horse campers. The chalet provides modern restrooms and shower facilities for campers. An RV dump station is also provided. A fee is charged for overnight camping.
>
> **Picnic Area:** Past the campground the picnic area features two shelters, picnic tables, and grills.
>
> **Water Recreation:** None.
>
> **Trails:** A hilly woodlands and prairie landscape awaits the horseback rider or hiker, who may enjoy 5 miles of trails during the summer. Skiers and snow-mobiles use the trails during the winter.
>
> **Recreational Facilities:** Playground equipment is provided in the picnic area. During the winter the ski hill comes alive for beginner and intermediate downhill skiing. The hill is served by a towrope, and equipment rental is provided at the chalet.

Seasons: The park trails are open year-round. The campground is open during the summer season and the ski hill is open during the winter.

Directions: From Ivanhoe, take U.S. Highway 75 south for 15 miles to U.S. Highway 14 in Lake Benton, turn right and go west; watch for the park signs on the left side of the road.

(To read more about the park, see "25 Favorite County Parks" in the first section of this guide.)

20. Norwegian Creek County Park

Norwegian Creek enters Lake Benton at the location of this park. It features a campground, picnic area, and lake access.

Camping: The campground includes 40 RV/tent sites, some of which have electricity and water, tables, fire rings, modern restrooms with showers, and an RV dump station. A fee is charged for overnight camping.

Picnic Area: Facilities include two shelters, picnic tables, and grills located near the beach.

Water Recreation: Two concrete boat ramps and a large sandy beach provide boating, fishing, and swimming access to Lake Benton.

Trails: A short hiking trail is provided on the park's 128 acres.

Recreational Facilities: None.

Seasons: The park is open from May through September.

Directions: From Ivanhoe, take U.S. Highway 75 south for 13.5 miles, then watch for and follow the park signs from Highway 75.

21. Picnic Point County Park

With over 40 acres of land on Lake Shaokatan, this park offers a quiet and peaceful retreat for outdoor enjoyment. It features camping, picnicking, and water-recreation opportunities.

Camping: The campground includes 30 RV/tent sites (12 with electricity and water), tables, fire rings, several vault toilets, and an RV dump station. A fee is charged for overnight camping.

Picnic Area: Facilities include a shelter, picnic tables, and grills.

Water Recreation: A concrete boat ramp, floating fishing pier, and sandy beach provide boating, fishing, and swimming access to Lake Shaokatan.

Trails: None.

Recreational Facilities: Playground equipment is provided near the picnic area.

Seasons: The park is open from May through September.

Directions: From Ivanhoe, take U.S. Highway 75 south for 5 miles to County Road 15, turn right and go west for 4 miles, following the park signs.

Lyon County

Parks and Fairgrounds
607 West Main Street
Marshall, MN 56258
(507) 629-4081
www.co.lyon.org/depts/publicworks/parks/

22. Garvin Park

Nearly 750 acres of hills, valleys, streams, and forest cover the landscape of Garvin Park in southern Lyon County. Garvin Park was originally dedicated in 1935, and it was named after H. C. Garvin, a Winona businessman, who donated funds and equipment to the park. Today, this park continues to welcome visitors

Garvin Park

looking for a quiet retreat from daily life.

Camping: Two separate campgrounds offer 30 RV/tent sites with electricity, vault toilets, modern restrooms with showers, and an RV dump station. A fee is charged for overnight camping, and a campground host lives on-site in the northern campground. The southern campground is designed to accommodate campers with horses.

Picnic Area: Three picnic areas include five large shelters, numerous picnic tables, grills, vault toilets, and various kinds of older-style playground equipment.

Water Recreation: The Cottonwood River flows through the middle of the park, offering a scenic landscape for picnicking and trail hiking.

Trails: There are a variety of trails within the park, including 2.5 miles of hiking trails, 5.5 miles of horseback riding/snowmobile trails, and 2.5 miles of skiing trails. A short hike to Merton's Lookout is worth the view from an observation tower.

Recreational Facilities: Softball fields, a winter sliding hill, and deer hunting (with bows) and turkey hunting seasons provide a variety of additional year-round opportunities.

Seasons: The park is open year-round.

Directions: From Marshall, take U.S. Highway 59 south for 13 miles.

(To read more about the park, see "25 Favorite County Parks" in the first section of this guide.)

Martin County

County Parks
201 Lake Avenue
Fairmont, MN 56031
(507) 238-3126
www.co.martin.mn.us

23. Bright Lake County Park

Located in southern Martin County, this is a small, natural-area park. It features a picnic area, trails, and lake access.

Camping: None.

Picnic Area: A small shelter and a couple of old tables and grills are provided.

Water Recreation: A concrete ramp provides access to Bright Lake.

Trails: A few hiking trails are provided.

Recreational Facilities: None.

Seasons: The park is open year-round.

Directions: From the junction of County Road 39 and Interstate 90 near Fairmont, take I-90 west for 6 miles to State Highway 263, turn left and go south on for 9 miles, then turn left and go 2 miles east on a gravel road; the park is on the left side of the road.

24. Cedar-Hanson County Park

Cedar-Hanson County Park features a variety of camping and day-use opportunities on approximately 80 acres of hardwood forest and lakeshore. It is comprised of two campgrounds and picnic areas located on Cedar Lake.

Camping: The southern campground features 12 RV/tent sites and three hike-in tent-camping sites, all located on the lakeshore. Portable toilets and handicap-accessible vault toilets are provided. The northern campground features 12 RV/tent sites and vault toilets (one that is handicap-accessible). A fee is charged for overnight camping, and a campground host lives on-site.

Picnic Area: The southern picnic area features a medium-sized shelter with picnic tables, grills, and a water pump. The northern picnic area includes a large shelter with several tables.

Water Recreation: Motorized and nonmotorized boating and fishing can be enjoyed on Cedar Lake. Facilities include a handicap-accessible fishing pier, a small dirt ramp, a concrete ramp, and a small swimming beach.

Trails: A few hiking trails are provided.

Recreational Facilities: Playground equipment is provided.

Seasons: The park is open from May through September.

Directions: From the junction of County Road 39 and Interstate 90 near Fairmont, take I-90 west for 12.5 miles to State Highway 4, turn right and go north for 9 miles, then turn left and follow the park signs.

25. Klessig Park

Klessig is a small wayside park south of Fairmont on Iowa Lake. Klessig has the distinction of being the southernmost county park in Minnesota because it is only a few feet from the Iowa border.

Camping: None.

Picnic Area: A few picnic tables and a fire ring are provided for picnicking.

Water Recreation: Fishing and boating on Iowa Lake is common, a concrete ramp with a dock provides access to the lake.

Trails: None.

Recreational Facilities: None.

Seasons: This park is open year-round.

Directions: From Fairmont, take State Highway 15 south for 10 miles, then turn right on County Road 41; the park is immediately on the left side of the road.

26. Perch Lake County Park

A quiet and peaceful setting characterizes the landscape of this park. It features a small campground, a picnic area, trails, and lake access.

Camping: The campground includes 4 RV/tent sites along with handicap-accessible restrooms with showers. A fee is charged for overnight camping, and a park caretaker lives on-site.

Picnic Area: A large shelter, picnic tables, and grills are provided

Water Recreation: Lake access is possible by carrying in a canoe or fishing

A shady playground overlooks East Chain Lake at Wolter Park.

from the shore.

Trails: Hiking and mountain-bike riding can be enjoyed on the trails that wind through the hardwood forest of the park.

Recreational Facilities: Facilities include playground equipment.

Seasons: The park is open from May through September.

Directions: From Fairmont, take State Highway 15 north for 10 miles, turn left and go west on 220th Street for 2 miles; follow the brown signs to the park entrance.

27. Timberlane County Park

This is a 50-acre natural-area park, which preserves the forested landscape between South Silver and Iowa lakes. It features a few trails and lake access.

Camping: None.

Picnic Area: None.

Water Recreation: A concrete ramp with a dock provides boat access to South Silver Lake.

Trails: A few hiking trails wind their way through the park.

Recreational Facilities: None.

Seasons: This park is open year-round.

Directions: From Fairmont, take State Highway 15 south for 10 miles, turn right on County Road 41, and go west for 1 mile; the park is on both sides of the road.

28. Wolter Park

This is a small, day-use park located on East Chain Lake in southeastern Martin County. It features a picnic area and lake access.

Camping: None.

Picnic Area: Picnickers will enjoy a small shelter, picnic tables, grills, and a fire ring. A portable toilet is also provided.

Water Recreation: Fishing and boating can be enjoyed on East Chain Lake. A small concrete ramp with a dock provides access to the lake.

Trails: None.

Recreational Facilities: A modern play structure is provided.

Seasons: The park is open from May through September.

Directions: From Fairmont take State Highway 15 south for 5 miles, then turn left on County Road 12 and go 5 miles east, watch for the park on the right side of the road.

Murray County

Parks and Fairgrounds
2500 28th Street
Slayton, MN 56172
(507) 836-6148
www.murray-countymn.com

29. Corabelle Park

This is a small, lake-access park located on Corabelle Lake.

Camping: None.

Picnic Area: Facilities include one shelter, a picnic table, and a vault toilet.

Water Recreation: A boat ramp provides boating and fishing access to the lake.

Trails: None.

Recreational Facilities: None.

Seasons: The park is open year-round.

Directions: From Slayton, take County Road 32 south, then west, for 4 miles, turn left and go south on State Highway 267 for 2 miles; keep going south as the road changes to County Road 4 and then County Road 31; go south on County Road 31 for 2.5 miles, then turn right and go west on County Road 1 for less than a mile; follow the park signs.

30. End-O-Line Railroad Park

Located on the north side of the City of Currie, this unique park celebrates the history of the railroad and pioneer life in Minnesota. Visitors can explore a historic railroad yard, complete with a locomotive, caboose, engine house, and a variety of other buildings, including a country school and a general store.

Camping: None.

Picnic Area: Picnickers can enjoy the use of picnic tables, a shelter, water, and handicap-accessible restrooms.

Water Recreation: None.

Trails: A short nature trail and birding area are provided. Bikers and hikers can also access the 6-mile-long, paved loop trail that connects this park with Lake Shetek State Park.

Recreational Facilities: A variety of railroad-themed playground equipment is provided.

Seasons: The park is open from Memorial Day through Labor Day.
Directions: From Slayton, take U.S. Highway 59 north for 5.5 miles, turn right and go east on State Highway 30 for 4 miles, then turn left and go north on County Road 38; watch for the park on the right side of the road in Currie.

31. Forman Acres

This is a small, lake-access park located on Lake Shetek adjacent to Shetek State Park.

Camping: None.
Picnic Area: Facilities include one shelter, picnic tables, and a vault toilet.
Water Recreation: A concrete boat ramp provides boating and fishing access to the lake.
Trails: None.
Recreational Facilities: None.
Seasons: The park is open year-round.
Directions: From Slayton, take U.S. Highway 59 north for 5.5 miles, turn right and go east on State Highway 30 for 4 miles, turn left and go north on County Road 38 for 2 miles, then turn left and go west on County Road 37 for 1.5 miles; follow the county park signs.

There's access to Lake Shetek at Foreman Acres.

32. Lake Sarah East

This is a small, lake-access park located on Lake Sarah. It includes a picnic area and a playground.

Camping: None.

Picnic Area: Facilities include one shelter, picnic tables, and a vault toilet.

Water Recreation: A concrete boat ramp provides boating and fishing access to the lake.

Trails: None.

Recreational Facilities: Playground equipment is provided.

Seasons: The park is open year-round.

Directions: From Slayton, take U.S. Highway 59 north for 11 miles; the park is on the left side of the road.

33. Lake Sarah West

A mixture of young and middle-aged trees and open areas characterizes the landscape of this small park. It includes a small campground, a picnic area, and lake access.

Camping: The campground features 10 RV sites with electricity, a grassy tent-

Lake Sara Park West accommodates RV camping.

camping area, tables, fire rings, an RV dump station, and vault toilets. A fee is charged for overnight camping.

Picnic Area: The picnic area features four shelters, picnic tables, grills, and water.

Water Recreation: A small beach, fishing pier, and concrete ramp provide swimming, boating, and fishing access to the lake. A handicap-accessible vault toilet is provided near the boat ramp.

Trails: None.

Recreational Facilities: Playground equipment is provided.

Seasons: The park is open from April through October.

Directions: From Slayton, take U.S. Highway 59 north for 10 miles, turn left and go west on County Road 16 for 2.5 miles, turn right and go north on County Road 30 for 1 mile, then turn right and go east on County Road 100.

34. Lime Lake Park

A small dam located at this park keeps a steady water level on Lime Lake. Visitors can also enjoy picnicking and lake-access opportunities.

Camping: None.

Picnic Area: The picnic area features one shelter, picnic tables, grills, and vault toilets.

Water Recreation: A fishing area near the dam and concrete ramp provides boating and fishing access to the lake.

Trails: None.

Recreational Facilities: None.

Seasons: The park is open year-round.

Directions: From Slayton, take U.S. Highway 59 southeast for 6 miles to County Road 6 to the edge of Avoca, turn right and go west on County Road 6; watch for a right turn and signs to the park and a cemetery.

35. Marsh's Landing

Located on Valhalla Island on Lake Shetek, this is a small, lake-access park. Lake Shetek is the largest lake in southwestern Minnesota and features a variety of water sports and pretty good fishing.

Camping: None.

Picnic Area: Facilities include one shelter, picnic tables, and vault toilets.

Water Recreation: A handicap-accessible fishing pier and two concrete boat ramps provide boating and fishing access to the lake.

Fish from shore or boat at Marsh's Landing.

Trails: None.

Recreational Facilities: None.

Seasons: The park is open year-round.

Directions: From Slayton, take U.S. Highway 59 north for 8.5 miles, turn right and go east on County Road 13 for 1.5 miles; the park is on the left side of the road after crossing the bridged causeway.

36. Seven Mile Lake Park

Located on the edge of the town of Fulda, on Fulda First Lake, this park offers a nice setting for outdoor enjoyment. It features camping, picnicking, and lake access.

    Camping: A small campground with eight RV sites and a grassy tent-camping area features electrical hookups, tables, fire rings, an RV dump station, and handicap-accessible restrooms with showers. A fee is charged for overnight camping.

Picnic Area: The picnic area features two shelters, picnic tables, grills, and water.

Water Recreation: A small beach and a concrete ramp provide swimming, boating, and fishing access to the lake.

Trails: None.

Recreational Facilities: A variety of playground equipment and ball fields are provided.

Seasons: The park is open from April through October.

Directions: From Slayton, take U.S. Highway 59 southeast for 12 miles to County Road 2 in Fulda, turn right and go to South Lafayette Avenue, turn left and follow it to the park.

37. Swensen Park

A grassy, open landscape provides plenty of space for camping and picnicking in this small park. It is 10 acres in size and located on Current Lake.

Camping: The campground features 20 RV sites with electricity, a grassy tent-camping area, tables, fire rings, an RV dump station, and vault toilets. A fee is charged for overnight camping.

Picnic Area: The picnic area features two shelters, picnic tables, grills, and water.

Water Recreation: A concrete ramp provides boating and fishing access to the lake.

Trails: None.

Recreational Facilities: Playground equipment and ball fields are provided between the picnic area and the campground.

Seasons: The park is open from April through October.

Directions: From Slayton, take State Highway 30 west for 4.5 miles to County Road 29, turn right and go north on County Road 29 for 12 miles, turn left and go west on County Road 20 for 2.5 miles, then turn left on State Highway 91; the park is on the right side of the road.

Nicollet County

Public Works Department
1700 Sunrise Drive
Saint Peter, MN 56082
(507) 931-1760
www.co.nicollet.mn.us

38. Seven Mile Creek Park

Located at the confluence of Seven Mile Creek and the Minnesota River, this park includes over 600 acres of beautiful forested landscape. It features a trout stream, access to the Minnesota River, and a scenic network of trails.

Camping: None.

Picnic Area: Facilities include three shelters, several picnic tables, and vault toilets (some of which are handicap-accessible).

Water Recreation: The Minnesota Department of Natural Resources stocks the creek with brown trout, so it is possible to fish within the park. Small-boat and/or canoe access and fishing access to the Minnesota River is also provided.

Trails: There are 8 miles of hiking and horseback-riding trails within the park. During the winter the trails are open for cross-country skiing.

Recreational Facilities: Two volleyball courts, a ball field, and playground equipment are provided.

Seasons: The park is open year-round.

Directions: From Saint Peter, take U.S. Highway 169 south for 4 miles.

Nobles County

Parks Department
960 Diagonal Road
Worthington, MN 56187
(507) 468-2224
www.co.nobles.mn.us/highway/parks/parks.htm

39. Adrian Spring County Park

Only one acre in size, this wayside park features Adrian Spring, once a frequent stop for early travelers who availed themselves of its water.

Camping: None.

Picnic Area: A couple of picnic tables are provided.

Water Recreation: None.

Trails: None.

Recreational Facilities: None.

Seasons: The park is open year-round.

Directions: From Worthington, take Interstate 90 west for 17 miles to State Highway 91 in Adrian, turn left and go south a short distance into Adrian, then turn right on County Road 35 and go west for 1 mile.

40. Fury Island County Park

The main part of this park is actually an island connected to the mainland by a narrow road. It is 10 acres in size and features a moderate-sized campground and a picnic area on East Graham Lake.

Camping: The developed campground features about 15 RV/tent sites with tables and fire rings and a modern restroom building with showers. Farther down the shoreline off the island, there are about eight dispersed campsites. A park caretaker lives nearby at Maka-Oicu County Park, and a fee is charged for overnight camping.

Picnic Area: Facilities include a large shelter, picnic tables, grills, and restrooms.

Water Recreation: Boating and fishing access to East Graham Lake is provided by a concrete ramp.

Trails: None.

Recreational Facilities: A playground is available for children.

Seasons: The park is open from May through September.

Maka-Oicu County Park

Directions: From Worthington, take State Highway 60 northeast for 8 miles to County Road 1, turn left and take County Road 1 north for 5.50 miles, then turn left and go west on County Road 16 for 2.50 miles; turn right and go north on County Road 55 for 1.50 miles. A vehicle permit is required for entry into the park.

41. Hawkeye County Park

Located on Indian Lake, this 40-acre park is relatively undeveloped and has been left in a natural condition. It features a scenic landscape of hardwood forest and rolling hills.

Camping: None.

Picnic Area: A picnic area exists and the grass is mowed, but the area is not currently equipped with tables or other amenities.

Water Recreation: A small dirt ramp provides boat access to Indian Lake.

Trails: None.

Recreational Facilities: None.

Seasons: The park is open year-round.

Directions: From Worthington, take County Road 5 south and east for 9.50 miles to 330th Street, turn left and go east for 1.50 miles, then take County Road 53 south for a half mile to the park entrance.

42. Maka-Oicu County Park

Located on West Graham Lake, this park offers a variety of recreational opportunities on a historic site. It features a large campground, a nice picnic area, and a sandy swimming beach.

Camping: Two developed campgrounds feature 40 RV/tent sites with tables, fire rings, and water. A modern restroom building with showers is located next to the picnic area and a large campground. Vault toilets are provided in the less-developed campground. A small, one-room cabin is also available for rental. A caretaker lives on-site, and fees are charged for overnight camping.

Picnic Area: Facilities include an extra-large shelter, picnic tables, grills, and restrooms.

Water Recreation: Boating, fishing, and swimming access to West Graham Lake is provided by a concrete ramp and a large swimming beach.

Trails: A few miles of trails wind through the natural landscape of the park.

Recreational Facilities: None.

Seasons: The park is open from May through September.

Directions: From Worthington, take State Highway 60 northeast for 8 miles to County Road 1, turn left and take County Road 1 north for 5.5 miles, then turn left and go west on County Road 16 for 2.5 miles; turn right and go north on County Road 55 for 3 miles. A vehicle permit is required for entry into the park.

43. Midway County Park

This is a 45-acre undeveloped park located on the site of an old gravel pit. Today the area is gradually returning to a natural condition.

Camping: None.

Picnic Area: None.

Water Recreation: None.

Trails: None.

Recreational Facilities: None.

Seasons: The park is open year-round.

Directions: From Worthington, take Interstate 90 west for 17 miles to State Highway 91 in Adrian, turn right and go north on State Highway 91 for 4 miles, then turn right and go east on County Road 14 for 1 mile; the park is on the left side of the road.

44. Sportsman County Park East

Located on the east end of Ocheda Lake, this is a seven-acre lake-access park.

Camping: None.

Picnic Area: None.

Water Recreation: A small dirt ramp provides boat access to Ocheda Lake.

Trails: None.

Recreational Facilities: None.

Seasons: The park is open year-round.

Directions: From Worthington, take County Road 5 south for 2.5 miles; the park is on the right side of the road.

45. Sportsman County Park West

Located on the west side of Ocheda Lake, this is a four-acre lake-access park.

Camping: None.

Picnic Area: None.

Water Recreation: A small dirt ramp provides boat access to Ocheda Lake.

Trails: None.

Recreational Facilities: None.

Seasons: The park is open year-round.

Directions: From Worthington, take U.S. Highway 59 south for 5 miles, then turn left and go east on County Road 6 for 1 mile.

46. Sunrise Prairie County Park

This is a 22-acre undeveloped park that contains a pioneer cemetery and a native grass prairie.

Camping: None.

Picnic Area: None.

Water Recreation: None.

Trails: None.

Recreational Facilities: None.

Seasons: The park is open year-round.

Directions: From Worthington, take Interstate 90 west for 10 miles to County Road 13, take it south for 8.5 miles to County Road 54, then turn right and go west on County Road 54 for 3 miles; the park is on the right side of the road.

Pipestone County

There are no county parks in Pipestone County.

Redwood County

County Courthouse
250 S. Jefferson
Redwood Falls, MN 56283
(507) 859-2491 (park phone)
www.walnutgrove.org/pcpark.htm

47. Plum Creek Park

Visitors to this park can enjoy 200 acres of oak and elm forest along Plum Creek, similar to what pioneer woman and author Laura Ingalls Wilder experienced during her youth. It features a large picnic area, a developed campground, trails, and a swimming beach.

Camping: Facilities include 60 RV/tent sites with electricity and handicap-accessible restrooms with showers. A fee is charged for overnight camping, and a caretaker is on duty.

Picnic Area: Both the upper and lower sections of the park have picnic areas that include shelters, picnic tables, grills, water pumps, and vault toilets. The upper area overlooks Lake Laura, while the lower area is nestled along the banks of the Plum Creek.

Water Recreation: Lake Laura is a small reservoir that provides swimming and fishing opportunities. A nice sandy beach supervised by lifeguards is located adjacent to the campground.

Trails: Opportunities include a short hiking trail around Lake Laura and hiking trails along Plum Creek.

Recreational Facilities: In the upper park there is a nine-hole Frisbee-disc-golf course and playground equipment, and in the lower park softball fields, volleyball courts, and playground equipment are provided.

Seasons: The park is open from May through September.

Directions: From Redwood Falls, take U.S. Highway 71 south for 19 miles to U.S. Highway 14, take that west for 16 miles to Walnut Grove; take County Road 20 west for 1 mile, then County Road 78 south for another mile.

(To read more about the park, see "25 Favorite County Parks" in the first section of this guide.)

Rock County

Highway Department
204 East Brown Street
Luverne, MN 56156
(507) 283-5010

48. Schoneman County Park

This roadside park features two small ponds and an open landscape that is perfect for wildlife observation. It is also carries the distinction of being the southwesternmost county park in the state.

Camping: None.

Picnic Area: Facilities include two shelters, picnic tables, grills, and portable toilets.

Water Recreation: Three small ponds and a handicap-accessible floating fishing pier provide fishing opportunities. A handicap-accessible portable toilet is provided near the fishing pier.

Trails: Some short hiking trails wind through the park.

Recreational Facilities: A wildlife observation tower provides a unique opportunity to see birds from a higher viewpoint.

Seasons: The park is open from April through October.

Directions: From Luverne, take U.S. Highway 75 south for 2 miles; the park is located on the left side of the road directly across from the Luverne Municipal Airport.

Watonwan County

Highway Department
710 Second Avenue South
Saint James, MN 56081
(507) 375-3393

49. Eagles Nest County Park

This park preserves a hardwood forest along the Watonwan River. It offers camping and hiking opportunities throughout the natural landscape.

Camping: Four grassy campsites are available with electrical hookups. A restroom and shower building is located adjacent to the campsites. A fee is charged for camping through a self-pay box. Backcountry campsites are located at various locations along the hiking trails.

Picnic Area: A large shelter and picnic tables are provided next to the campsites.

Water Recreation: The Watonwan River offers some fishing opportunities.

Trails: Several miles of hiking and skiing trails wind their way through the forest and along the river.

Recreational Facilities: None.

Seasons: The campground is open from May through September, and the trails are open year-round.

Directions: From Saint James, take State Highway 30/60 east for 5 miles, watching for the county park sign; be prepared to turn left and go north for three-quarters of a mile, following the signs.

50. Kansas Lake Park

This is a small, lake-access park that includes a fishing pier and picnic area.

Camping: None.

Picnic Area: Picnic tables and a small shelter are provided.

Water Recreation: A handicap-accessible fishing pier offers an opportunity for shoreline fishing, and a concrete ramp with a dock provides access to Kansas Lake.

Trails: None.

Recreational Facilities: None.

Seasons: The park is open year-round.

Directions: From Saint James, take State Highway 4 south for 4 miles, then turn right, following the signs to the county park.

No doubt about it—kids love county parks!

51. Long Lake Park

This is a small, day-use park located on Long Lake in south-central Watonwan County. It features a picnic area and a swimming beach.

Camping: None.

Picnic Area: A small shelter, picnic tables, and portable toilets are provided.

Water Recreation: Swimmers will enjoy a small sand beach, while a public access boat ramp next to the park provides access to Long Lake.

Trails: None.

Recreational Facilities: None.

Seasons: The park is open from May through September.

Directions: From Saint James, take State Highway 4 south for 6 miles, then turn left on County Road 10; the park entrance is immediately on the left side of the road.

Southeast Region

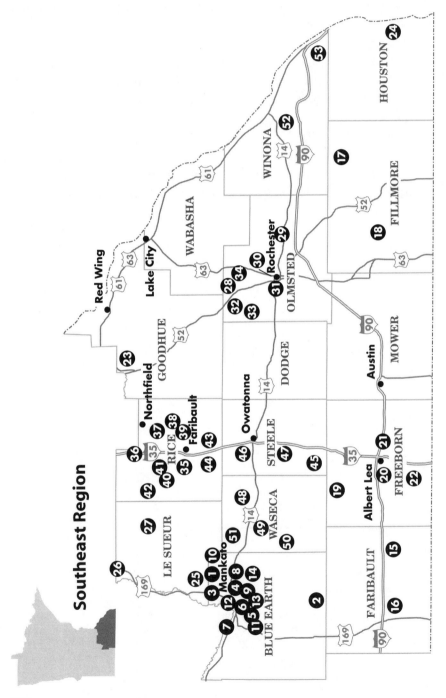

SOUTHEAST REGION

Park Department
35 Map Drive
Mankato, MN 56001
(507) 625-3282
www.co.blue-earth.mn.us/dept/parks

1. Bray Park

Bray Park is nearly 100 acres in size and located on the east side of Madison Lake. It offers opportunities for tent and RV camping, picnicking, swimming, and hiking.

Camping: The campground includes 33 RV sites and 10 tent sites. Facilities include a handicap-accessible restroom/shower building and an RV dump station. A fee is charged for overnight camping, and a caretaker lives on-site.

Bray Park offers camping, swimming, and hiking on the shores of Madison Lake.

Picnic Area: A large shelter, picnic tables, and grills are available to accommodate several picnickers. In addition, a small, log-cabin-style picnic shelter is available by reservation.

Water Recreation: A double concrete boat ramp with a dock, a handicap-accessible fishing pier, and an unsupervised swimming beach provide boating, fishing, and swimming opportunities on Madison Lake. The swimming beach includes restrooms, a changing house, a deck, and tables.

Trails: A handicap-accessible nature trail nearly 1-mile long provides a firsthand glimpse at the outdoor environment. The trail continues on for an additional three-quarters of a mile as a narrow footpath.

Recreational Facilities: A modern play structure and volleyball court are provided.

Seasons: The campground is open from April through October.

Directions: From Mankato, take U.S. Highway 14 southeast for 9.5 miles, turn left and go north on County Road 48 for 3 miles; the park entrance is on the left.

2. Daly Park

This is another large, camping-friendly park in Blue Earth County. In fact, it is the largest campground in the Blue Earth park system. A beautiful lakeshore landscape and well-designed facilities make it an enjoyable park to visit.

Camping: The campground features 15 tent sites, 71 RV sites, handicap-accessible restrooms and showers, and an RV dump station. A fee is charged for overnight camping, and resident caretakers live on-site.

Picnic Area: Shelters, picnic tables, and grills are provided for visitor enjoyment.

Water Recreation: Lura Lake offers plenty of fishing, boating, and swimming opportunities. Lake access includes a double concrete boat ramp with a dock, a handicap-accessible floating fishing pier, and a swimming beach.

Trails: A short, half-mile nature trail explores a unique island.

Recreational Facilities: Modern playground equipment, horseshoes, tennis courts, and volleyball courts are provided.

Seasons: The campground is open from April through October.

Directions: From Mankato, take State Highway 22 south for 18 miles to County Road 7 in Mapleton, take County Road 7 south for 3.5 miles to County Road 191, turn right and go west for 2 miles; watch for the park entrance sign.

Duck Lake Park

3. Duck Lake Park

Duck Lake is a popular summer day-use area located in northeast Blue Earth County. It features a large, sandy beach, a picnic area, and canoe/paddleboat rentals.

Camping: None.

Picnic Area: A large shelter, picnic tables, and grills are provided. Additional facilities include handicap-accessible restrooms. A caretaker lives on-site during the summer season.

Water Recreation: A large swimming beach is the focal point of this park. Duck Lake offers boating, fishing, and swimming opportunities. A dirt boat ramp with a dock is provided. Paddleboat and canoe rentals are also available.

Trails: None.

Recreational Facilities: Modern playground equipment is provided.

Seasons: The park is open from April through October.

Directions: From Mankato, take U.S. Highway 14 southeast for 8 miles, turn left and go north on State Highway 60 for 3.5 miles, then turn left and go north on County Road 187 for less than one mile; the park is on the right side of the road.

4. Lake George Park

This is a small, day-use park located on the south shore of Lake George. It features a beach and picnic area.

Camping: None.

Picnic Area: Picnic tables and grills are provided. The existing restroom fa-cilities are not usable.

Water Recreation: Lake George offers boating, fishing, and swimming oppor-tunities. Water facilities include a swimming beach and a concrete boat ramp.

Trails: None.

Recreational Facilities: A modern playground structure is provided.

Seasons: The park is open from April through October.

Directions: From Mankato, take U.S. Highway 14 southeast for 5.5 miles to County Road 17, turn left and continue east on County Road 17 for a quarter mile, turn left and go north on County Road 27 for 4 miles, then turn right and go east on County Road 187 for a few feet; the park is on the left side of the road.

5. Rapidan Dam Park

This 32-acre park is located on the Blue Earth River and has a natural hardwood forest and river bluff landscape. It is named after the nearby power dam and features hike-in campsites.

Camping: Twenty hike-in tent campsites are located along the river and offer a primitive camping experience. Sanitary facilities include three portable

The Blue Earth River winds through Rapidan Dam Park.

toilets; one is handicap-accessible. Water is also available. A fee is charged for overnight camping, and a park caretaker works in the Rapidan store/office.

Picnic Area: A shelter with picnic tables is provided.

Water Recreation: Carry-in canoe access to the river is provided. Shoreline fishing is also a popular activity.

Trails: The campsites along the river are connected by a hiking trail.

Recreational Facilities: Modern playground equipment is located next to the shelter.

Seasons: The park is open from April 1 to November 1.

Directions: From Mankato, take U.S. Highway 169 south for 10 miles to County Road 9, turn left and go east on for 1.5 miles; the park entrance is on the left side of the road.

(To read more about the park, see "25 Favorite County Parks" in the first section of this guide.)

6. Red Jacket Park

This small day-use park provides access to the Red Jacket bicycle trail. The nearby renovated railroad trestle is a unique feature.

Camping: None.

Picnic Area: A picnic shelter, picnic tables, and a portable toilet are provided.

Water Recreation: Carry-in canoe access to the Le Sueur River is provided.

Trails: The Red Jacket paved recreation trail goes right by the park and is connected to Mankato.

Recreational Facilities: None.

Seasons: The park is open year-round.

Directions: From Mankato, take State Highway 66 south for 2.5 miles; the park is on the left side of the road.

7. Williams Nature Center

This 65-acre nature park overlooks the Minnesota River near Mankato. An interpretive center building is available for large group gatherings and family functions.

Camping: None.

Picnic Area: The interpretive center building has facilities for indoor picnics.

Water Recreation: None.

Trails: One-and-a-half miles of paved-surface, self-guided nature trails, two scenic overlooks, and restrooms are provided.

Recreational Facilities: None.

Seasons: The heated interpretive center building is available year-round.
Directions: From Mankato, take State Highway 68 west for 3 miles and follow the signs.

WAYSIDE AREAS: Blue Earth County maintains four wayside areas that provide water access and picnicking opportunities in natural settings.

8. Eagle Lake Wayside

Camping: None.
Picnic Area: None.
Water Recreation: A concrete ramp with a dock provides boat access to Eagle Lake.
Trails: None.
Recreational Facilities: None.
Seasons: The park is open year-round.
Directions: From Mankato, take U.S. Highway 14 east for 4 miles, turn left and go north on County Road 3/186 for 2 miles, then turn right and go east on County Road 26 for 1 mile; the rest area is on the right side of the road.

9. Hungry Hollow Stop

Camping: None.
Picnic Area: A shelter and picnic tables are provided.
Water Recreation: Canoeing on the Le Sueur River is popular. A carry-in canoe launch is provided.
Trails: None.
Recreational Facilities: None.
Seasons: The wayside is open from April through October.
Directions: From Mankato, take State Highway 22 south for 7 miles to County Road 15, turn left and take County Road 15 for 1 mile to the wayside, which is located on the left side of the road.

10. Lone Pine Rest Area

Camping: None.
Picnic Area: None.
Water Recreation: Boating and fishing can be enjoyed on Madison Lake. A dirt boat ramp and floating fishing pier are provided.
Trails: None.

Recreational Facilities: None.

Seasons: The park is open year-round.

Directions: From Mankato, take U.S. Highway 14 east for 9.5 miles, turn left and take County Road 48 north for 2 miles; the rest area will be on the left side of the road.

11. Watonwan Stop

Camping: None.

Picnic Area: A picnic shelter and tables are provided.

Water Recreation: The Watonwan River offers fishing and canoeing opportunities. A small-boat or canoe access is provided.

Trails: None.

Recreational Facilities: None.

Seasons: The wayside is open from April through October.

Directions: From Mankato, take U.S. Highway 169 south for 16 miles, then follow the brown signs to the rest area.

CONSERVATION AREAS: Blue Earth County maintains three natural conservation areas for the preservation of open space, nature study, and wildlife observation.

12. Indian Lake Conservation Area

This unique area features 120 acres of restored wetlands and a nature trail.

Camping: None.

Picnic Area: None.

Water Recreation: None.

Trails: Hikers, horseback riders, and wildlife watchers can enjoy a 1-mile-long nature trail.

Recreational Facilities: None.

Seasons: This area is open year-round.

Directions: From Mankato, take County Road 66 south for 2 miles and then follow the signs.

13. Schimek Park

This natural area contains a 30-acre mixture of hardwood forest and open areas.

Camping: None.

Picnic Area: Picnickers will find a shelter and picnic tables available for use.

Water Recreation: The Maple River provides fishing opportunities.

Trails: A short nature trail winds through the park.

Recreational Facilities: None.

Seasons: This area is open year-round.

Directions: From Mankato, take State Highway 66 south for 12.5 miles to County Road 10, turn left and go east for 1 mile, then watch for the sign.

14. Wildwood Park

This area consists of nearly 30 acres along the Le Sueur River.

Camping: None.

Picnic Area: None.

Water Recreation: The Le Sueur River provides numerous fishing opportunities.

Trails: A short nature trail is provided.

Recreational Facilities: None.

Seasons: This area is open year-round.

Directions: From Mankato, take State Highway 83 east for 6 miles, then continue east on County Road 184 for 1 mile, turn right and go south on County Road 28 for 1 mile; the entrance is on the right side of the road.

Dodge County

There are no county parks in Dodge County.

Faribault County

Highway Department
415 North Main
Blue Earth, MN 56013
(507) 526-3291
www.co.faribault.mn.us

15. Pihls Park

Originally built as a private retreat, this area was donated to Faribault County in the 1960s for use as a park. Today, visitors come to camp and enjoy a 20-acre park. It makes a nice destination or rest stop while traveling on Interstate 90.

Camping: The campground features 30 RV sites with electricity and a tent area. Each site has a table and a fire ring. Handicap-accessible restrooms with showers, drinking water, and an RV dump station are provided. Fees are charged for camping and dump-station use. A park caretaker lives on-site.

Picnic Area: The picnic area features two shelters, picnic tables, and grills.

Water Recreation: Rice Lake is a shallow lake that offers boating, fishing, and nature observation opportunities. A handicap-accessible fishing pier is located in the park. Canoes and kayaks can be carried in to the lake, and a boat ramp is located nearby.

Trails: A short nature trail follows the lakeshore.

Recreational Facilities: Playground equipment, a modern play structure, and a Frisbee-disc golf practice course are provided.

Seasons: The park is open from May 1 to October 1.

Directions: From Blue Earth, take Interstate 90 east for 20 miles to State Highway 22, turn right and go south for a half mile, then continue south on 560th Avenue for another half mile.

16. Woods Lake Park

Woods Lake Park is tucked away near the Iowa border in the rolling farm fields of southern Faribault County. It features a quiet campground and a sandy swimming pond, all on nearly 40 acres.

Woods Lake Park

Camping: The campground features 20 RV sites with electricity and 10 tent sites. Each site has a table and a fire ring. Restrooms, showers, drinking water, and an RV dump station are provided. Fees are charged for camping and dump-station use. A park caretaker lives on-site.

Picnic Area: The picnic area features an extra-large shelter, numerous picnic tables, and grills. Restrooms are provided near the beach.

Water Recreation: Woods Lake is a small pond formed by a manmade retaining wall on a small stream. The result is a nice swimming hole with a large sandy beach. A restroom/bathhouse is provided next to the beach.

Trails: None.

Recreational Facilities: Older-style playground equipment, a volleyball court, and basketball courts are provided.

Seasons: The park is open from May 1 to October 1.

Directions: From Blue Earth, go south 7 miles on U.S. Highway 169, turn right and go west 1 mile, turn right and go north following the park signs; the park entrance road is on the left side of the road.

Fillmore County

County Courthouse
101 Fillmore Street
Preston, MN 55965
(507) 765-4566
www.co.fillmore.mn.us

17. Bucksnort Park

This is a small wayside park located in a quiet river valley. It is a nice location to fish for trout, a popular activity in this part of Minnesota.

Camping: Camping in the park is allowed by permit only. Permits can be obtained from the sheriff's department. No facilities are provided.

Picnic Area: Facilities include a shelter and two picnic tables.

Water Recreation: Trout Run Creek is a designated trout stream and offers some fishing opportunities.

Trails: None.

Recreational Facilities: None.

Seasons: The park is open year-round.

Directions: From Preston, take U.S. Highway 52 north for 5.5 miles, turn right

Fish a designated trout stream at Bucksnort Park.

and go east, then north, on County Road 11 for 7 miles, turn right and go east on State Highway 30 for 1 mile; the park is on the left side of the road.

18. Masonic Park

Masonic Park is off the beaten path, located in a valley and featuring an open, grassy area. A unique limestone rock cliff is an interesting land feature located across the creek from the park.

Camping: Camping in the park is allowed by permit only. Permits can be obtained from the sheriff's department. No facilities are provided.

Picnic Area: Facilities include a shelter and picnic table, but they are not maintained.

Water Recreation: Deer Creek offers some fishing opportunities.

Trails: None.

Recreational Facilities: None.

Seasons: The park is open year-round.

Directions: From Preston, take State Highway 16 west for 14 miles to County

Masonic Park

Road 38, turn right and go north on County Road 38 for 4 miles; take the second gravel road on the right side and go down the hill to the park.

Freeborn County

Highway Department
3300 Bridge Avenue
Albert Lea, MN 56007
(507) 377-5188

19. Arrowhead Point County Park

Arrowhead Point County Park preserves and protects a large peninsula on Freeborn Lake. A thick hardwood forest covers the park's landscape and provides a relaxing atmosphere for outdoor recreation.

Camping: None.

Arrowhead Point County Park juts out into Freeborn Lake.

Picnic Area: Two picnic areas feature one large shelter with electricity, three small shelters, picnic tables, grills, a water pump, and vault toilets.

Water Recreation: Freeborn Lake surrounds the park on three sides. Shoreline fishing and a dirt ramp provide boat and fishing access.

Trails: A 1-mile-long walking trail starts at the park entrance and winds through the park to the end of the peninsula.

Recreational Facilities: Older-style playground equipment is provided.

Seasons: The park is open from May through September.

Directions: From Albert Lea, go 6 miles north on State Highway 13 to County Road 25, turn left and go 4.5 miles west on County Road 25, then turn right and go 1 mile north on County Road 8; the park entrance road is on the left side of the road.

20. Pickerel Lake County Park

This is a small, scenic roadside park located on a knoll overlooking Pickerel Lake. It provides a relaxing place to stop for a wayside rest or picnic under the shade of several large oak and elm trees.

Camping: None.

Picnic Area: The picnic area has one medium-sized shelter, picnic tables, grills, a water pump, and vault toilets.

Water Recreation: Boat and shoreline fishing access is possible within the park. A dirt ramp can accommodate canoes and small boats.

Trails: None.

Recreational Facilities: None.

Seasons: The park is open from May through September.

Directions: From Albert Lea, go 2 miles south on U.S. Highway 69; the park is on the right side of the road.

21. Saint Nicholas Park

This park area preserves the historic site of the Saint Nicholas Village on Albert Lea Lake. The village was founded in 1856 and was the first settlement in Freeborn County. Today, it features a wooded lakeshore and picnic area.

Camping: None.

Picnic Area: Two small picnic areas with tables are located in two different locations in the park.

Water Recreation: Albert Lea Lake can partially be seen through the trees in the park, but direct access to the lake is not possible due to steep banks.

Pickerel Lake County Park

Saint Nicholas Park preserves the site of a historic village on Albert Lea Lake.

Trails: A short walking trail connects the two picnic areas.

Recreational Facilities: None.

Seasons: The park is open year-round.

Directions: From Albert Lea, go 2 miles east on County Road 19; the park is on the left side of the road.

22. White Woods County Park

White Woods County Park offers a variety of day-use and picnic activities for residents and visitors to southern Freeborn County. Beyond the developed picnic area, it is primarily maintained in a natural condition.

Camping: None.

Picnic Area: The picnic area has one large shelter and two small shelters. Picnic tables, grills, fire rings, a water pump, and vault toilets are also provided.

Water Recreation: Lower Twin Lake can be accessed by hiking trails.

Trails: A few miles of hiking trails are provided.

Recreational Facilities: None.

Seasons: The park is open from May through September.

Directions: From Albert Lea, go 8 miles south on U.S. Highway 69; just south of Twin Lakes, the park entrance is on the right side of the road.

Goodhue County

County Government Center
509 West 5th Street
Red Wing, MN 55066
(651) 385-3000

23. Lake Byllesby County Park

Located on the south shore of the Lake Byllesby reservoir in the far-northwestern corner of the county, this small park provides a variety of day-use activities. It features a large swimming beach, and a frequently used concrete ramp is available to access the lake for boating and fishing.

Camping: None.

Picnic Area: Facilities include a medium-sized picnic area with picnic tables, grills, water, and an open-air shelter.

Water Recreation: Lake Byllesby is a reservoir that provides motorboating, canoeing, kayaking, sailing, and fishing opportunities. A concrete boat ramp is provided in the park. The park also features a large, sandy swimming beach.

Trails: None.

Recreational Facilities: A small playground and two volleyball courts are provided.

Seasons: The park is open from May through September.

Directions: From Cannon Falls, take County Road 19 for 1.5 miles to the park entrance, on the right side of the road.

Houston County

County Courthouse
304 South Marshall
Caledonia, MN 55921
(507) 725-5822
www.co.houston.mn.us

24. Wildcat Park

Located in bluff country on the shoreline of the Mississippi River, this park is the southeasternmost of any of the county parks in Minnesota. It features two boat ramps, a campground, and a picnic area for visitor use.

Camping: Facilities include about 20 RV/tent sites with electricity, tables, fire rings, an RV dump station, vault toilets, and a concessions building/office with modern restrooms and showers. A fee is charged for overnight camping.

Picnic Area: Facilities include two shelters, picnic tables, grills, water, and vault toilets.

Water Recreation: Double concrete boat ramps provide boating and fishing access to the Mississippi River. A fee is charged for overnight parking.

Trails: None.

Recreational Facilities: None.

Seasons: The park is open from May through September.

Directions: From Caledonia, take County Road 3 east for 14 miles, turn right and go south on State Highway 26; watch for the park entrance on the left side of the road.

Le Sueur County

County Parks
88 South Park Ave.
Le Center, MN 56057
(507) 357-2251

25. Lake Washington Park

With over 150 acres of forest and 500 feet of shoreline, this park offers a nice setting for lakeside picnics or gatherings. It features a picnic area, trails, and a conference center building.

Camping: None.

Picnic Area: Facilities include picnic tables and a conference center building that has modern restrooms.

Water Recreation: Fishing is possible from the Lake Washington shoreline or the small dock provided.

Trails: Around 3 miles of hiking trails are provided.

Recreational Facilities: None.

Seasons: The park is open year-round.

Directions: From Le Center, take State Highway 99 southwest for 6 miles to County Road 15, take it south for 2.5 miles, take County Road 18 west for 4 miles; take County Road 19 south for 1.5 miles, then take County Road 103 east for a half mile.

26. Ney Center Park

Over 400 acres of forest, prairie, creeks, ravines, and historic farmsteads are a part of the landscape of this park and the accompanying Wilhelm Ney Wildlife Preserve. The Ney Environmental Education Foundation was formed to develop and carry out the mission of educating young people about the environment, utilizing the preserve/park as a natural classroom.

Camping: None.

Picnic Area: An interpretive building serves as the center for classes and public programs. The center can also be rented for meetings and events, and it features several seating arrangements and handicap-accessible restrooms. For information regarding the programs at the center call (507) 665-6244.

Water Recreation: None.

Trails: A self-guided nature trail leads visitors around a pond.

Recreational Facilities: None.

Seasons: The park is open year-round for scheduled activities.

Directions: From Le Center, take State Highway 112 west for 8.5 miles, then north for 6.5 miles, through Le Sueur, to U.S. Highway 169; take 169 north for 5.5 miles to County Road 19, turn left and take County Road 19 west for 1.5 miles, then go south on Nature Center Road.

27. Richter's Woods Park

The landscape of this park includes 80 acres of natural forest. The only developments are a short trail and an old renovated barn that now serves as a meeting center and picnic pavilion.

Camping: None.

Picnic Area: The refurbished barn features picnic tables and modern restrooms, and it can be reserved for large groups.

Water Recreation: None.

Trails: A short, 1-mile-long hiking trail is provided.

Recreational Facilities: None.

Seasons: The park is open year-round.

Directions: From Le Center, take State Highway 99 east for 6 miles, take County Road 161 north for 3 miles, then take County Road 163 north for a half mile.

Mower County

There are no county parks in Mower County.

Olmsted County

Public Works Department
2122 Campus Drive SE
Rochester, MN 55904
(507) 285-8231
www.olmstedpublicworks.com

28. Allis Park

Allis Park provides boat access near the Lake Shady Dam. A small parking lot and concrete boat ramp are provided on the water's edge.

Camping: None.

Picnic Area: None.

Water Recreation: Fishing and boating opportunities are provided by a small-boat ramp access to Lake Shady.

Trails: None.

Recreational Facilities: None.

Seasons: The park is open year-round.

Directions: From Rochester, take U.S. Highway 52 north for 9.5 miles to County Road 12 (Oronoco exit), go east for a half mile, then turn right on County Road 18 and go south for a half mile; the park is on the right side just before the bridge.

29. Chester Woods Park

Completed in 1994, this is a newer county park located a few miles east of Rochester. It features over 1,300 acres of hardwood forest, native prairie, streams, and a small lake.

Camping: Facilities include 52 RV/tent sites, 37 sites with electricity, handicap-accessible restrooms with showers, water, and an RV dump station. A fee is charged for overnight camping, and a park caretaker lives on-site.

Picnic Area: Seven picnic shelters that feature picnic tables, grills, and water are provided.

Water Recreation: Chester Lake provides swimming, fishing, and canoeing opportunities. Gasoline motors are prohibited on the lake. A swimming beach with a changing house, handicap-accessible fishing piers, and a canoe rental service are provided.

Trails: Hikers and horseback riders can enjoy 15 miles of trails. Eight miles of trail are groomed for skiing in the winter.

Recreational Facilities: Two playground structures are provided, and one is handicap-accessible.

Seasons: The park is open year-round for day use, and the campground is open from May through September.

Directions: From Rochester, take U.S. Highway 14 east for 7 miles; the park is on the right side of the road. A vehicle permit is required for entry into the park. (*To read more about the park, see "25 Favorite County Parks" in the first section of this guide.*)

30. Graham Park

Graham Park is actually the Olmsted County Fairgrounds. This site includes a grandstand and various other buildings used for county fair activities as well as to host other large special events throughout the year.

Camping: None.

Picnic Area: None.

Water Recreation: None.

Trails: None.

Recreational Facilities: None.

Seasons: The park is open during special events.

Directions: This park is located in Rochester at the intersection of U.S. Highway 63 and 12th Street.

31. Mayowood Corridor

The Mayowood Corridor is approximately 75 acres of green space along the Zumbro River in southwest Rochester. A paved trail is the only developed feature of this recreation area. Nearby is Mayowood, the exquisite mansion built in 1911 by Charles Mayo, one of the founders of the world-famous clinic that bears his family's name.

Camping: None.

Picnic Area: None.

Water Recreation: None.

Trails: A paved trail provides biking, hiking, and skiing opportunities.

Recreational Facilities: None.

Seasons: The trail is open year-round.

Directions: In Rochester, take 16th Street, turn west and take Mayowood Road SW out past the historic Mayowood Mansion; access to the trail is provided shortly after crossing the river.

32. Oronoco Park

Located only minutes from busy Highway 52, Oronoco Park offers travelers a nice place to take a rest stop. A historical marker on the site describes the Oronoco Gold Rush. Gold was assumed to be found on the Zumbro River, and locals had aspirations of Oronoco becoming a boomtown. The reports of gold turned out to be false.

Camping: Facilities include six tent campsites with picnic tables, fire pits, grills, and drinking-water faucets. A small restroom building with vault toilets and showers serves the campground and picnic area. A park caretaker is located on-site.

Picnic Area: The picnic area overlooks the lake and offers several picnic tables and an open-air pavilion.

Water Recreation: Lake Shady provides a scenic backdrop for picnicking and fishing opportunities.

Trails: None.

Recreational Facilities: A large, modern play structure is provided.

Seasons: The park is open from May through September.

Directions: From Rochester, take U.S. Highway 52 north for 9.5 miles to County Road 12 (Oronoco exit), then go east for a quarter mile; the park entrance is on the right side of the road.

33. Oxbow Park

Oxbow Park features over 500 acres of forest, streams, and fields, as well as the "oxbow" features of past stream channels for which this park is named. Oxbows are formed when a stream channel changes, leaving a small section of channel as a small pond separate from the stream. The Oxbow Nature Center and a small zoo also provide unique opportunities for visitors.

Camping: The campground features several RV/tent sites, water, and restrooms. A fee is charged for overnight camping, and a park caretaker lives on-site.

Picnic Area: Two picnic areas feature picnic tables, grills, four shelters, water pumps, and handicap-accessible vault toilets.

Water Recreation: None.

Trails: Hikers will enjoy nearly 7 miles of trails.

Recreational Facilities: Playground equipment is provided in the main picnic area.

Seasons: The park is open from May through September.

Directions: From Rochester, take U.S. Highway 14 west for 8 miles to County

Road 5 at Byron, turn right and go north for 3 miles on County Road 5, turn right on County Road 4 and immediately left on County Road 105; follow County Road 105 to the park.

34. White Bridge Fishing Access

The White Bridge Fishing Access offers fishing opportunities for kids, adults, and people of all abilities on the Zumbro River. The remnants of a former bridge now serve as a scenic setting for enjoying outdoor activities and fishing.

Camping: None.

Picnic Area: A small picnic area with a fire ring is located adjacent to the fishing access. A handicap-accessible satellite toilet is provided.

Water Recreation: The scenic Zumbro River is wide at this spot and provides boating and fishing opportunities. Two small, handicap-accessible fishing decks provide shoreline fishing access. A private boat ramp and restaurant are located next to the park.

Trails: None.

Recreational Facilities: None.

Seasons: The park is open year-round.

Directions: From Rochester, take U.S. Highway 52 north for 9.5 miles to County Road 12 (Oronoco exit), go east on County Road 12 for 3 miles (look for the Fishing Access sign), turn north on County Road 118 (White Bridge Road NW); the park is at the end of this road.

Rice County

Department of Parks and Building Maintenance
320 NW Third Street
Faribault, MN 55021
(507) 332-6105
www.co.rice.mn.us

35. Ackman Park

Lakeside fishing opportunities are provided at this small park. It is located on a strip of land between Wells and Cannon lakes.

Camping: None.

Picnic Area: None.

Water Recreation: Shoreline fishing can be enjoyed on either lake from the shoreline or a fishing pier.

Trails: None.

Recreational Facilities: None.

Seasons: The park is open from May through October.

Directions: From Faribault, take State Highway 60 southwest for 2 miles, then turn right and go west on County Road 12 for 1 mile.

36. Albers Park

This is a small day-use park located on Union Lake in northern Rice County. Visitors can enjoy picnicking, lake access, or fishing at this location.

Camping: None.

Picnic Area: Facilities include a pavilion, a general picnic area, picnic tables, grills, and modern restrooms.

Water Recreation: Fishing can be enjoyed on the lakeshore or from a fishing pier. A canoe access to Union Lake is also provided.

Trails: A short trail connects the picnic area to the fishing pier.

Recreational Facilities: Playground equipment is provided.

Seasons: The park is open from May through October.

Directions: From Faribault, take Interstate 35 north for 12 miles to the County Road 19 exit, go west on County Road 19 for one quarter mile, then turn left and go south on County Road 46 for 1 mile.

37. Cannon River Wilderness Area

Over 800 acres of the Cannon River valley's hardwood forest is preserved within this area, which is located between Faribault and Northfield. A majority of the area remains undeveloped and offers a remote and quiet outdoor experience. Besides summer, the remainder of the year is also enjoyable, with bright, colorful leaves in fall and a blanket of snow in winter.

Camping: Four primitive campsites are provided.

Picnic Area: Facilities include a shelter, a general picnic area, picnic tables, a water pump, and vault toilets.

Water Recreation: Fishing and canoeing can be enjoyed on the Cannon River. A carry-in canoe access is provided.

Trails: Hikers and skiers will enjoy a variety of opportunities, including 5 miles of trails and a self-guided nature trail. A large footbridge provides access to both sides of the river.

Recreational Facilities: None.

Seasons: The park is open year-round.

Directions: From Faribault, take State Highway 3 north and follow the park signs; the wilderness area begins about 4 miles northeast of Faribault.

38. Caron Park

This park features a landscape of forest and prairie plant communities that offer a unique location for nature observation. Hiking trails provide easy access for nature study or outdoor enjoyment.

Camping: None.

Picnic Area: A shelter, picnic area, picnic tables, water pump, and vault toilet are provided.

Water Recreation: None.

Trails: One-and-a-half miles of hiking trails are provided within the park.

Recreational Facilities: None.

Seasons: The park is open from May through October.

Directions: From Faribault, take State Highway 60 east for 5 miles, turn left and go north on County Road 23 for 3 miles, then continue north on County Road 88 for 1 mile.

39. Falls Creek Park

Sixty acres of hardwood forest and a creek are the highlights of this park. It is located only minutes from downtown Faribault and features hiking and skiing trails.

Camping: None.

Picnic Area: A shelter, picnic tables, grills, a water pump, and a vault toilet are provided.

Water Recreation: None.

Trails: A few miles of hiking trails and a nature trail provide opportunities to enjoy the natural environment of the park.

Recreational Facilities: None.

Seasons: The park is open from May through October.

Directions: From Faribault, take State Highway 60 east for 1 mile.

40. Heron Island

Heron Island is located on Shields Lake and provides wildlife habitat for birds. Nature observers might be able to catch a glimpse of a great blue heron or an American egret from a distance. Since it is a bird habitat, public access is not allowed.

Camping: None.

Picnic Area: None.

Water Recreation: None.

Trails: None.

Recreational Facilities: None.

Seasons: Public access to the island is not allowed.

Directions: From Faribault, take State Highway 21 northwest 9 miles to Shields Lake.

41. Hirdler Park

This small park features opportunities for picnicking and lake access. It is located on Mazaska Lake northwest of Faribault.

Camping: None.

Picnic Area: Facilities include a shelter, picnic tables, grills, and a vault toilet.

Water Recreation: A concrete boat ramp provides boating and fishing access to Mazaska Lake.

Trails: None.

Recreational Facilities: A modern play structure, horseshoe pits, and basketball and volleyball courts are provided.

Seasons: The park is open from May through October.

Directions: From Faribault, take State Highway 21 northwest for 7 miles.

42. Kalina Park

This is a small park located on Phelps Lake in northwestern Rice County. It provides lake and fishing access from the shoreline and a fishing pier.

Camping: None.

Picnic Area: None.

Water Recreation: A fishing pier provides fishing opportunities on the lake.

Trails: None.

Recreational Facilities: None.

Seasons: The park is open from May through October.

Directions: From Faribault, take State Highway 21 northwest for 14 miles to Kent Avenue, turn right and go north on it for 2 miles, then turn left and go west on Cody Lake Trail for a half mile.

43. King Mill Park

This is a small park located in Faribault very close to Interstate 35. It is a nice location for a quiet rest stop when traveling through the area. It features a scenic picnic area near the King Mill Dam.

Camping: None.

Picnic Area: Facilities include a shelter, picnic tables, and handicap-accessible restrooms.

Water Recreation: A fishing pier is provided on the Cannon River.

Trails: None.

Recreational Facilities: None.

Seasons: The park is open from May through October.

Directions: From Interstate 35 in Faribault, take State Highway 60 east for less than a mile.

44. Shager Park

Located just west of Faribault, this is a nice lakeside park. It features a developed shoreline that offers trail access and several water-based recreation activities including swimming, boating, and fishing.

Camping: None.

Picnic Area: Facilities include a shelter, two general picnic areas, picnic tables, grills, and a vault toilet.

Water Recreation: Swimming, boating, and fishing access to Cannon Lake is provided by a beach, a boat ramp, and two fishing piers. A bathhouse building is provided at the beach.

Trails: Access to the multiple-use, paved Sakatah Singing Hills State Trail is provided. The Sakatah State Trail is also used by snowmobiles during the winter.

Recreational Facilities: Volleyball posts are provided.

Seasons: The park is open from May through October.

Directions: From Faribault, take State Highway 60 west for 2 miles.

Steele County

Parks and Recreation Department
PO Box 57
Owatonna, MN 55060
(507) 451-1093
www.co.steele.mn.us/scparks/parksindex.html

45. Beaver Lake County Park

This 17-acre park provides a variety of outdoor opportunities on a small lake in

Beaver Lake County Park

the southwest corner of Steele County. A walking path tunnel under the County Road connects the picnic area and swimming beach of the park.

Camping: None.

Picnic Area: Two picnic pavilions with tables and grills are available for reserved or drop-in use. Restrooms and a handicap-accessible portable toilet are also provided.

Water Recreation: A large, sandy swimming beach is supervised by lifeguards during the summer months, while a concrete ramp provides access to Beaver Lake. A handicap-accessible fishing pier offers those without boats the opportunity to fish from shore.

Trails: A few trails wind through the forested part of the park.

Recreational Facilities: A modern play structure, sand volleyball court, and horseshoe pits are provided.

Seasons: The beach is open from June through August, while the park is open year-round for lake access.

Directions: From Owatonna, go south on Interstate 35 for 9 miles to the Hope exit, turn right on County Road 4 and go west for 1 mile, turn left on County Road 14 and go south and west for 5 miles, turn right on County Road 21 and go west for 2 miles, then turn left on County Road 28 and go 1 mile; the park is located on both sides of County Road 28.

46. Crane Creek County Park

This park preserves the site of the Crane Creek School, a one-room schoolhouse that operated from 1915 to 1968. The school is no longer standing, but visitors can enjoy the park as a nice rest stop along Highway 14.

Camping: None.

Picnic Area: A small picnic shelter includes picnic tables, grills, and electricity amenities and can be reserved with a deposit fee. A portable toilet is provided from May until October.

Water Recreation: None.

Trails: None.

Recreational Facilities: None.

Seasons: The park is open from April through October.

Directions: From Owatonna, go west on U.S. Highway 14 for 3 miles; the park is on the right side of the highway.

47. Hope School County Park

The Hope Schoolhouse is preserved as the central part of this small park. It is available for a meeting space or large group gathering rentals.

Camping: None.

Picnic Area: Picnic tables and outdoor activities are provided. A portable toilet is provided outside from May until October. Restrooms are available inside when the schoolhouse is rented.

Water Recreation: None.

Trails: None.

Recreational Facilities: A grassy ball field and older-style playground equipment are provided.

Seasons: The park is open year-round.

Directions: From Owatonna, go south on Interstate 35 for 9 miles to the Hope exit, turn right and go 1 mile on County Road 4, turn right and go 1 mile into the small town of Hope; the park is on the right side of the road.

Wabasha County

There are no county parks in Wabasha County.

Waseca County

County Parks
307 N. State Street
Waseca, MN 56093
(507) 835-0590
www.co.waseca.mn.us/parks.htm

48. Blowers Park

Blowers Park is comprised of 76 acres of trees and wetlands. It provides an ideal habitat for wildlife and a beautiful setting for picnicking only minutes from Waseca. Picnicking, lake-access facilities, and trails are provided for visitor use.

Camping: None.

Picnic Area: A medium-sized shelter, picnic tables, grills, and a handicap-accessible vault toilet are provided.

Water Recreation: A carry-in access on the edge of Watkins Lake accommodates canoes and small boats. Fishing and waterfowl hunting are other opportunities available from this access.

Trails: A few short walking trails can be found in the park.

Recreational Facilities: A modern play structure is provided.

Seasons: The park is open year-round.

Directions: From Waseca, go 3.5 miles north on County Road 4; the park is on the right side of the road.

49. Courthouse Park

With its 175 acres, Courthouse Park is the flagship park of the Waseca County Park System. Winding trails and the scenic shoreline of the Le Sueur River make this an enjoyable destination for outdoor recreation.

Camping: Sixteen primitive campsites are provided and are only accessible by trail from the parking lot. Six sites are designated for horseback riders and reservations are required for every site. A fee is charged for camping.

Picnic Area: Three picnic shelters, several tables, grills, a water pump, fire rings, and vault toilets are provided. One vault toilet is handicap-accessible.

Water Recreation: Scenic, 50-foot-high bluffs frame sections of the Le Sueur River as it winds its way through the park.

Trails: Several miles of trails provide hiking, horseback riding, snowmobiling, and skiing opportunities. A short, paved, handicap-accessible nature trail is designed for self-guided tours.

Recreational Facilities: Older-style playground equipment, volleyball courts, and a ball field are provided.

Seasons: The park is open year-round.

Directions: From Waseca, go 3 miles south on County Road 4, then turn right and go west on County Road 75 for 1 mile; the park entrance is on the right side of the road.

50. Eustice Park

Eustice Park features 50 acres of hardwood forest along the Little Cobb River. It features a picnic area and a few trails.

Camping: None.

Picnic Area: Facilities include a small shelter, picnic tables, grills, a water pump, and a handicap-accessible vault toilet.

Water Recreation: None.

Trails: A few short trails are provided for horseback riding or hiking.

Recreational Activities: Older-style playground equipment is provided.

Seasons: The park is open year-round.

Directions: From Waseca, take County Road 4 south, then west, for 14 miles to State Highway 83; look for the park signs and follow them to the park entrance.

51. Okaman Park

This is a small day-use park located on Lake Elysian, which is the largest lake in Waseca County. It features carry-in lake access and picnic facilities.

Camping: None.

Picnic Area: A small shelter, picnic tables, grills, and a portable toilet are provided.

Water Recreation: A carry-in access on the edge of Lake Elysian accommodates canoes and small boats for fishing and boating opportunities.

Trails: None.

Recreational Facilities: None.

Seasons: The park is open year-round.
Directions: From Waseca, take State Highway 13 north for 5 miles to County Road 22, turn left and go 5.5 miles west on County Road 22, go 2.5 miles west on County Road 35, then turn left and go 1 mile south on County Road 5; the park is on the right side of the road.

UNDEVELOPED PARKS: Waseca County has been active in setting aside parks throughout the county. Ten additional parks covering a total of 220 acres have been designated but left undeveloped. These parks provide wildlife habitat and nature study areas for future generations. Some are accessible while others are surrounded by private lands. Since they have no developed facilities and some are difficult to access, I did not do any further research on these parks for this guidebook.

Winona County

Planning Department
177 Main Street
Winona, MN 55987
(507) 457-6335
www.co.winona.mn.us

52. Farmers Community Park
This park was originally dedicated for public use by H. C. Garvin in 1925. It features a scenic valley setting along the Garvin Brook. Garvin, a Winona businessman, also helped established Garvin Park in Lyon County.
Camping: None.
Picnic Area: Facilities include nine open shelters, three enclosed shelters, numerous tables, grills, water pumps, and vault toilets.
Water Recreation: Garvin Brook is a designated trout stream and provides fishing opportunities.
Trails: None.
Recreational Facilities: Two modern play structures and various other playground equipment are provided.
Seasons: The park is open from April 30 through October 1.
Directions: From Winona, take U.S. Highway 14 west for 9 miles; watch for the park entrance on the left side of the road.

A stone gate greets visitors to Farmers Community Park

53. Apple Blossom Overlook Park

This scenic park features over 50 acres of hardwood forest, prairie, and wildlife habitat on top of the bluffs overlooking the Mississippi River Valley. The park is currently undeveloped; however, future plans include picnic areas, trails, scenic overlooks, and an interpretive center.

Camping: None.

Picnic Area: A small gravel parking lot provides access to the park area.

Water Recreation: None.

Trails: None.

Recreational Facilities: None.

Seasons: The park is open year-round.

Directions: From Winona, take State Highway 43 south for 6 miles, turn left and go east on Interstate 90 for 13 miles; take the County Road 12 exit, turn left and go south on County Road 12 for 2 miles; then turn left and go east on County Road 1 for 5 miles; the park is on the left side of the road.

INDEX